THE JOY OF TRUE MEDITATION

Words of Encouragement
for Tired Minds and Wild Hearts

Jeff Foster

NSP

UNITED KINGDOM

Publisher's Note

The material provided in this book is intended to offer helpful information on the subjects discussed. This book is not meant to be used, nor should it be used, to diagnose or treat any medical condition. It is sold with the understanding that the publisher is not engaged with rendering psychological, financial, legal, or other professional services. If expert assistance or counseling is needed, the services of an appropriately competent professional should be sought.

THE JOY OF TRUE MEDITATION
First English edition published May 2019 by New Sarum Press

© Jeff Foster 2019
© New Sarum Press 2019

Cover Image: *Exercise at Sunrise* by Jennifer Willis Photography
Back cover portrait by Emily Scher:
www.emilyscherphotography.com
Layout and design: Julian Noyce

ISBN:978-1-9993535-3-7

New Sarum Press | 6 Folkestone Road | Salisbury | SP2 8JP
United Kingdom

For Dad. You did it *Your Way*.

Contents

Life has a simple and fiercely kind invitation for us: to be *as we are* the in the face of *what is.*

True meditation, an easily disappearing yet well-worn path on the journey home to ourselves, is both difficult to define and predictably trustworthy in its unfolding. It encompasses a genuine encounter with *all of who we are,* as well as *all of who we take ourselves to be that won't hold up in the light of honest, compassionate inquiry.* The path unfolds along essential lines, along emotional and existential crevices and outcroppings that life displays within and around us.

To accept the invitation to this essential journey home requires courage. Oddly enough, sometimes that courage shows up as a desperation, a surrender, an up-giving… or as total and complete 'cowardice' as we can't bear to look, to feel, to experience whatever is here.

And yet, here we still are. Asleep, awake, leaning in, leaning out, encountering this present moment.

Just as we are.

True meditation is vividly relational. It is an ultimate encounter with what is real: with a clear, direct seeing of truth in any form in our lives. This clear seeing of what is present—be it an emotion, a thought, a misperception, a moment of joy, or the deepest essence of things—is a relational, intimate gesture. This gesture invites us to embody a warm, holding presence, an unflinching capacity to fundamentally welcome and be all of the beautiful muck and mess of the human life. It is deeply intimate and leaves nothing out. It forsakes nothing, and includes everything. *The moment itself contains within it the seeds of all we need to meet the moment.*

As we meet and welcome whatever comes, feeling our breath, bodies, the pulsing existence at our core, we *become* welcoming itself. We discover, as we *lean in*, that this welcoming presence is essential to who we are.

The clear seeing that comes from this kind of radical welcoming presence can usher in with it compassion, ease, shocking insight, laughter, loss of a sense of self and prior orientations, and relief. Deep relief—from the game, trap or prison of our minds. As we lean in to our breath, feelings, emotions, sensations, and thoughts, we discover things aren't as we thought they were. The fear is less scary than it seems, the anger less threatening. Our disowned, unwanted, unloved parts begin to come home, to be just as they are in a space that does not refuse them. We offer them a place in our heart, mind, and being that is free from the violence of self-refusal. *Even self-refusal is welcomed*; in fact, all inner violence and struggle, in the act of being welcomed as is, now encounters the true meaning of nonviolence. As we come home to ourselves in this way, we begin to rest.

I've taught mindfulness meditation around the world to United Nations humanitarian and development workers, to prison inmates, to Google employees, to military veterans. I can't find a single difference in the essential needs we all share, or in our collective capacity to both hide from and deeply encounter what is real. What I have seen and experience in myself and in others is that we share a longing for this simple welcoming presence in which to meet our tenderness, vulnerabilities, hopes, and fears. In the simple offering of our own presence, so much happens.

Meditation offers the hope, the salve, of the end of suffering. It just doesn't come to us like we want it to, or thought it would. It comes in the surrender into and through all that we experience, *including* our own deep suffering. There is good news: a deep trust arises as we embrace this path. We learn, whether over time, or because we have no other choice but to learn quickly and suddenly, that trust comes in each step, each breath, each plunge we take into the present moment without our former scaffolding. It's like falling back into your friends' arms without looking— it's scary but deep down you know you will have a soft landing. The truth of things, the rawness and reality of life in all of its display, becomes far safer, far softer, than our ideas ever were. The fear, the anger, the heartache may not leave, but they may transform in the presence of our love, becoming portals into the deep wise heart: the one we have perhaps long since abandoned.

This book is a relational gesture, a vulnerable sharing, a hand held out on the path, a strong treatise on the power of our very presence, breath, and the simplicity of being *all of who we are* in the face of all that each moment brings. Jeff weaves us into and out of every corner the mind creates to defend against the simplicity of this moment, displaying the tapestry in all its fullness so we're sure to remember that life is so much wilder and more free than we could ever have imagined.

These thoughtfully and bravely written pages include many invitations: to our aloneness, to our freedom, to our deep rest which we may have so long held at bay. His words beckon us to find a home within ourselves, to fall in love with our minds and bodies for perhaps the very first time. The prose is fierce, wild, passionate, poetic, unapologetic. Jeff's gentle words undo the stigma of trauma and provide breathing space to what we have made so *wrong* and *bad* within ourselves. He is agnostic in his fascination: he leaves nothing out. The sweat, tears, blood, shame, the dark impulses, the power and joy. All are included.

Hidden in each of this book's vignettes is a constant reminder of the fierceness and totality of the moment as an invitation to presence, to breath, back home. Jeff's invitations are manifold and pay homage to the pulsing, alive heart, and to the vital, inspired breath. By being who he is: a poet, lover, and madman in the best sense of the word, Jeff offers words of encouragement whispered into our tired ears and minds, meant for our dazzled, wild hearts to receive.

—Kelly Boys
Author of *The Blind Spot Effect: How to Stop Missing What's Right in Front of You.*
www.kellyboys.org

Some say the world

is a vale of tears,

I say it is

a place of soul-making.

—John Keats

THE DISCOVERY OF TRUE MEDITATION

I'd like to share with you a little of my story. It is a story that begins with death and ends with life and tells of the discovery of *true meditation*: not through books, spiritual teachers or meditation classes, but through death and rebirth, through venturing into the darkness of myself, through coming a hair's breadth from suicide and self-destruction, through breaking through the veil of dualistic mind to an inextinguishable inner Light. A Light that had been there all along. The Light of meditation. The Light of Oneness. The Light of my true self.

Mine is a story perhaps not dissimilar from your own. I believe we are all ultimately on the same journey back home... to the present moment. To the here and now.

From as early as I can remember, I believed that there was something profoundly *wrong* with me. I felt sick and broken and ugly inside; unworthy of love, a mistake of a human being; damaged beyond redemption, beyond hope. The terror of abandonment, and with it the terror of death itself, lurked deep within my bones and made me afraid and ashamed to live. I walked through the streets hunched over, hiding my face. I would never make eye contact with anyone for more than an instant; I was convinced they would flee in disgust if they saw into me.

I was exhausted all the time, profoundly tired on a very deep soul level. Entire school holidays I would spend hiding in my bedroom, numbing myself with computer games, movies and food, and generally longing for *a different life*. I ached and had tensions all over my body, which I saw as an enemy and was repulsed by.

I had secret panic attacks but told no-one. I had few friends, nobody to really talk to. I was bullied badly at school and hid in the restrooms during break times. I would come home drenched in sweat and stuff myself with chocolate and microwave hamburgers to try and numb the pain. I wore extra layers of clothing, even in the hottest days of summer, to soak up my excessive anxious perspiration.

I had no idea if I was male or female, straight or gay, man or beast, saint or murderer. Maybe there had been some huge mistake, and I had been born at the wrong moment, on the wrong planet, orbiting the wrong sun. Sometimes I didn't even know whether I was alive or dead. My identity was a giant question mark to me, and that disturbed me to my core.

As I got older, an urge to die grew within me. I fantasised often about killing myself or destroying the world or both. An ancient grief and rage boiled inside, yet I numbed it and put on a brave face. I excelled academically and was often top of the class at school. At eighteen, I was accepted into Cambridge University, a great honour for the family. I pretended to be happy, fulfilled, untroubled, easy-going, the archetypal "good boy". I gave no indication to the world as to the depths of my despair.

In my quiet moments during the day and in nightmares while sleeping I heard monsters moaning from deep within, terrible cries of forgotten selves I had buried in the blackness, abandoned parts of the psyche calling for love and help and attention from the Underworld.

I had given up on all my hopes and dreams. From an early age I had wanted to tell stories, make movies, inspire people, maybe even change the world, but I was petrified of failure and rejection, and dreaded my shameful insides being seen, and so I blocked off these risky creative passions. I lived outside of my body and outside of the present moment and in the fantasy world of the time-bound conceptual mind, in daydreams and nightmares, in convoluted philosophies and distant worlds, in pasts and futures, and always, always in regret and anticipation. I was homeless, divided from my true sanctuary and place of refuge. I had become separated from God, alienated from the Life Source, wrenched from the Divine Mother.

I ached with a cosmic loneliness I could not find a way to extinguish.

Later in my life, I came to the point of suicide. It seemed like the only solution to my impossible problem of living. I was exhausted beyond my ability to tolerate and I'd had enough of pretending, trying to 'fit in', living in a world that couldn't see me or didn't want me as I was. Something in me just wanted to *rest* from the exhausting project called "being a person in the world".

Of course, I didn't really want to die. Secretly, *I wanted so badly to live*. I just didn't know how. Nobody had ever shown me.

I believed physical death was the only way forwards.

I fell into a great darkness.

And then, one ordinary day, all my defences against life, all my resistance to being alive, all my conditioned protection against the pain and pleasure of raw experience, started to break down.

All the repressed unconscious material, all the thoughts and feelings and desires I had held down in order to appear 'normal' and 'civilised' started leaking, then pouring, then gushing into conscious awareness. Pandora's Box had broken open inside of me. I could no longer run from the darkness within, no longer push life away and seek refuge in the conceptual mind; there was no longer any safe haven to be found there. I was being called to *face life*. The joy, the terror, the rage, searing feelings of abandonment suppressed since childhood, waves of unspeakable grief—I could no longer escape them now. Raw trauma had been unleashed inside, everything held-back was now rushing into me, like an unstoppable torrent of *life*! I thought I was going to die, convinced that I would not be able to tolerate the intensity of it all for another moment.

But I did not die. In fact, I was beginning to heal. The old, unhappy 'me' was beginning to break down. My *no* to life was burning up and my true self was coming alive. Something deep inside me was starting to say *yes*—*yes* to being alive, *yes* to not knowing, *yes* to the joy and the sorrow of existence, *yes* to the mess of being an imperfect human being, *yes* to the darkness and the light, *yes* to all of it!

Over the next weeks and months, I came out of my mind and into the heart. I touched Presence, the Now, a profound Oneness with all things. I breathed. I could feel my heart again. I could feel the Sun on my face. Hear new sounds. Taste my food. See new horizons, new possibilities. Feel new sensations stirring in my body. I felt like a baby, experiencing the world for the first time. This sense of *being alive* was so intense sometimes, I thought it would kill or damage or at least overwhelm me, or perhaps send me spiralling into a void I would never escape from.

But feelings are always safe. It is our defences that hurt so much.

I will say that again. *Our feelings are safe, no matter how intense they are.* It is our *tensing-up* around our human feelings, our rejection and refusal of them, our unconscious efforts to destroy and annihilate and purify them inside of us, our shaming of our vulnerable inner life and the smothering of the inner child, which causes so much pain and suffering. Not the feelings themselves.

Instinctively, I began to *breathe through* all my 'unbearable' feelings, thoughts, desires. One moment at a time, I was able to bear these 'monsters', survive them, tolerate them, allow them, even make friends with them. And when I couldn't allow them, when the resistance felt too huge, when the inner rage felt volcanic, when grief came in waves and seemed like it could tear me apart, I felt something bigger bearing these energies, holding them, allowing them, something ancient and strong and infinite and eternal and loving and wholly unknowable to the mind. **Even when the moment seemed unbearable, I could always bear it. Something inside me was indestructible. It could not be killed. It was soft, vulnerable, radically open and receptive, but it was also stronger and harder and more valuable than the most precious diamond, and brighter than a billion suns.** I was beginning to discover my true nature; who I really was, before I had been taught to distrust myself, before the self-hatred and fearful conditioning, before the Fall. I was discovering my true identity as Presence-Awareness itself. As the Light that never goes out. As the Love that never dies. The great inextinguishable Fire within.

At the core of my separation-shame-abandonment-death wound, new hope was born. At the heart of duality, nonduality. In the midst of darkness, in the belly of the beast, new life. A resurrection. A forgiveness, a second chance. A new beginning.

Some days I quaked and convulsed with fear, all the fear I'd never really let myself feel, I let it move through me finally, instead of pushing it away. Some days I raged at the sky and the oceans and mountains, spoke all the words of the inner child who'd never had a voice before, words that weren't "nice" or "spiritual" or "kind", but raw and feral and wild and authentic and thrilling to speak. Oh, to hear myself speak my own, authentic words at last! I wept every day for about a year, wept out all the tears I'd never been able to weep as a child, all the tears I had stifled so as not to upset or anger or alienate anyone around me. I laughed like a baby sometimes, giggled until I could hardly breathe, often for no reason at all. Some days I felt ecstatic joy and terrible despair *in the very same moment*. I was a glorious mess! A wild, inconsistent, unpredictable and uncontrollable mess! There was so much room in me now. So much life. So much space. Sometimes I thought I was going mad, with all this freed-up energy moving inside. Some days I thought about checking myself into a mental hospital. But maybe we have to go 'insane' to heal. Maybe 'normality' or 'conformity' was the disease I'd been suffering from my whole life. Maybe the straitjacket of 'adaptation' was finally burning up in a fever of healing. And I was learning to trust myself again. Learning to stay close to my own experience, without judging it, without trying to fix it, without trying even to be free from it.

I was learning *true meditation* from the fiercest meditation teacher of all. Life itself.

I survived the death-rebirth process, began to be able to tolerate previously intolerable thoughts and feelings. And I gained new strength, found new courage, touched inner resources I never knew I had.

I started to fall in love with life again on this strange planet called Earth. All of life, the joy and the sorrow too, the boredom and the confusion, the disappointment and the doubt and the longing and the loneliness. All was sacred now. All was beloved and fascinating to me, like it had been when I was very young. I no longer wanted to be free from my feelings, *I wanted to feel them all, experience them all, taste them all.* I was no longer afraid of my thoughts, *I wanted to think up entire universes, create entire galaxies of imagination.* I was an artist again, as I had been when I was very young, in love with all of creation, seeing life through new eyes, eyes full of innocence and wonder. I was a vast ocean of Consciousness, learning to love all of the waves of thought, feeling, sensation…

I wanted to be broken and whole at the same time. I wanted the positive *and* the negative of existence too. I wanted the bliss but also the heartache. I wanted the expansion but I also wanted the contraction. I wanted the "up" but I also wanted the "down" of life. I wanted desire and lack of desire. I wanted feeling and I wanted to feel the absence of feeling too. I was hungry for all polarities of being. The yin and the yang. The comedy and the tragedy. The agony and the ecstasy. The storm and the sunshine. The flaws and the imperfections and the unbearable perfection of it all; I wanted all of myself, the mess and the miracle, the dirt and the stars. I wanted wholeness. Yes, not happiness but *wholeness*, a gift far greater than the mind's limited notion of happiness.

Day by day, moment by moment, breath by breath, I began to show myself to others. Let them see me. All of me.

I started to speak my truth. Shaking, sweating, heart pounding, dry mouth sometimes, nauseated sometimes, deeply embarrassed and ashamed to speak my truth, but I spoke it. The raw, wild, messy, inconvenient truth of myself.

Some 'friends' disappeared. Some stayed. New friends, new family, arrived, a new tribe that wanted the new me in all of my divine mess. They wanted me to say the wrong thing, make mistakes, show awkward feelings, speak inconvenient words, and they wanted to try and love me for it.

Somewhere along the line I found the courage to start writing about my 'awakening'. My dance with death and surrender to life and loss of 'the old me'. My pathless path to where I had always been. Word by word, line by line, paragraph by paragraph, I started to tell my deepest spiritual truth. I felt fear and trembling doing it at first—after all, I was not a writer, and often had no idea what I was writing or how to put words to this pre-verbal experience of love for all creation, but something deeper was guiding me, some benevolent and ancient force, giving me language, putting words to silence, pulling me onwards. A blog was published, then a book, then one day I found myself in front of a small group of people in someone's living room, talking about what I'd discovered: Presence. Deep Acceptance. This non-dual reality, this loving field where every thought and feeling is no less than divine. Where even our urge to die contains intelligence, consciousness, life. *Me, who'd been the most frightened person on Earth, sharing with others from the depths of my heart! How unexpected!* Soon I was talking to thousands of people all over the world in meetings and retreats, in one-to-ones and even online broadcasts, never knowing what I'd say, but trusting this inner voice anyway; never knowing what to teach or how to help, but allowing this ancient teaching to flow through the open and transparent channel of myself. Without a plan, without a clue about what I was doing, the path unfolded in front of me, step by step, moment by moment, and the role of 'teacher' was born—although I have never really seen myself as a teacher, more like a friend and ally. Someone who's not trying to fix or heal you. Someone who just wants to meet you as you are. Someone who's here to remind you of something you've always known.

I find myself writing these words to you now, dear reader, a transmission directly from my heart to yours. What an epic journey it has been, *back to the utter simplicity of this moment, back to the Garden of Eden,* to this unique instant of life, the place we inhabited before we innocently stepped away into the sorrows of time. Through the detritus of myself, through the sewage of the Underworld, through the gateway of terror and ego-death, and back into the eternal Now. The more I have learned to befriend, embrace and soothe my own sorrow, bliss, loneliness, anger, fears, my weird desires and wild uncontrollable urges, learned to love all the crazy voices in my head (without confusing them with reality), the more I have been able to accept and not fear them in you (and therefore be able to be present with you, and not try to fix you, but love you instead, exactly as you are). Your longings are my own. Your terrors have moved through me too. Your bliss and your despair move me deeply; they are so familiar here. Your burning questions are so recognizable and honest. Your doubts and uncertainties shine with life. *I have found a great compassion for humanity by meeting my own pain. I have found a great compassion for others by first finding compassion for myself.*

Throughout all of my struggles, I had never been alone, for a single moment. There was never anything wrong with me, and there is never anything wrong with you. We are not born into sin, only a forgetting. We are taught to hate ourselves. We can un-learn this self-aggression. We can un-forget. We can remember what we always knew. We can heal from the most profound self-loathing and fear of living. We can recover from even the most horrific depression. At the very heart of our hopelessness, there is new hope, rooted not in the mind and its images, but in the reality of Presence itself.

The healing journey is not about "getting rid" of the unwanted and "negative" material within us, purging it until we reached a perfect and utopic "healed state". No. That is the mind's version of healing. Healing is not a destination. True healing involves *drenching that very same 'unwanted' material within us with love, presence and understanding.* It involves penetrating our deepest shadows, our physical and emotional pains, those regions we have withdrawn from in fear and in loathing, with a *merciful and compassionate awareness.* Re-inhabiting those disavowed, rejected, forgotten and frightened regions, those abandoned realms of the body and mind, with curious attention in the present moment. *For what we attend to, we can love.*

What we see as 'wrong' within us, our fear, our doubt, our loneliness, is just a part of us calling for our tender attention, like a baby crying for her mother —then screaming, then wailing, until she receives what she wants. Love. It is *love*—kind, mindful, non-judgemental, warm and curious awareness—that truly heals even our deepest wounds. Throughout this book I invite you in so many ways, through words and through the silences between them, back to this tenderness, back to this gentle and non-shaming way of meeting ourselves, back to this radical self-love, a self-love that is synonymous with meditation.

If you already have a formal meditation practice, I hope the reflections in the following pages inspire and help deepen your practice, and perhaps help you to see some things you've been missing. If you are new to meditation, if you have never meditated before, wonderful! We are all new to meditation if truth be told, because meditation just means looking with fresh eyes, being aware and awake to *what is*, flushing our embodied experience with attention, and this can only *ever* happen in the newness of the present moment. **You can drop into this space of meditation wherever you are and whatever you are doing.** On the bus or train, or resting cross-legged and eyes-closed in your living room, walking through the forest or through a shopping centre, or sitting on a park bench or in a doctor's waiting room. You can do it alone or you can do it with others. Every moment of your life, there is always the wonderful possibility to slow down, breathe deeply, and get curious about where you are. To begin again, to see life through the eyes of *not knowing*. To stop thinking about your life in the abstract, to stop seeking some other state or experience or feeling, to stop running towards another moment, and really fully experience **this unique instant of existence.**

Let us journey together now, back into the richness of ordinary life. Step by step, breath by breath, heartbeat by heartbeat, through our joy and our gladness, through our aches and pains, depressions and longings and ecstasies, through our deepest wounds, through the cracks in the heart, leaving behind all ideas of how we 'should' be, letting go of other people's guidebooks and self-help books and holy books, incinerating our second-hand, inherited maps of reality, and lovingly illuminating *our own first-hand, real-time, authentic experience* in the fire of present awareness.

This is true meditation, the kind of meditation that can save your life:

Pure fascination with this moment, exactly as it is.

If we will be quiet and ready enough,
we shall find compensation
in every disappointment.

- Henry David Thoreau

1. THE MIRACLE OF BREATHING

In any moment of our lives, we can become aware of our breath. It is our most wonderful anchor to Now.

Wherever we are, whatever time it is, whatever is happening in the external world, we can become curious about the breath's deep mystery, we can touch its life-giving rising and its falling too, its ascent and its descent. We can come out of our minds, drop out of the thought-constructed narrative of past and future, and touch the freshness and creativity of a single breathing moment.

Just for a moment, be present with the breath as it rises and falls, surges and descends at its own pace. As you read these words, attend to the sensations in your belly and chest, without trying to control or change them, and without trying to breathe in any kind of special way. Notice the rising and falling sensations, that very familiar wave-like ascent and descent of the chest and belly that has been with you, so close and so familiar, since you were a child. Where do you feel the rising and falling sensations the most strongly? Can you spend a few precious moments following them with your attention, *up and down, up and down?*

Let the breath be as it is. Rising and falling, rising and falling, like a wave in the ocean. Don't try to alter the breath. If the breath is shallow, let it be shallow. If it is deep, let it be deep right now. If it feels tight and restricted, or smooth and spacious, just be with that too. Don't try to make the breath into something that it's not. Don't compare today's breath with yesterday's or tomorrow's. Be with the breath as it is, in this moment, at this hour, on this day.

Just let the breath be natural. Let the body breathe itself. Soften any sense of holding around the breath, let it rise and fall in its own way, at its own pace.

See! For a moment, as you *pay attention to what's here* (and don't pay attention to what's not here) you are not caught up in the thought-constructed story of your life! For a moment, you have dropped out of the mind, the complex and dramatic narrative called 'me and my life', and into the living body. You have left the known world of habit and conditioning, and descended into the Unknown, into a great living Mystery.

And if you lose yourself again in the madness of the world, you can always ask the breath for help.

You can invoke the great and timeless question, "Breathing, how are you doing, right now?"

You can touch the mysterious 'Breathing One' inside with the greatest tenderness and fascination.

And notice, ultimately you are not doing the breathing: *you are being breathed.*

2. HOW TRUE HEALING HAPPENS ⫸

In childhood, many of us learned that certain feeling states, sensations in the body, urges and impulses within us, thoughts, desires and wants, were *not okay* to experience, let alone express. We were taught to fear and reject parts of ourselves, see them as 'dark' or 'negative' or 'dirty' or 'sick' or even 'sinful'. We were taught to distrust ourselves, distrust *the present moment*. We were made to believe that we were separate from all things, divided from the Whole. We were made to eat from the tree of knowledge of good and evil, digest dualistic conditioning from the world around us, swallow second-hand ideas and concepts of how we 'should' be. This was our innocent Fall from Grace. It wasn't our fault. We didn't know any better.

As young girls we may have been taught that our desires and our anger, our frustration and resistance and defiance, our sexual urges and fantasies were not okay—they were not natural, they were bad, or sick, or sinful, or dangerous, or shameful, or "not ladylike". As boys we may have been taught that it wasn't okay to be sad, or express our vulnerability, fears and doubts and heartaches and longings. That it wasn't okay to ask for help or have a need or express a boundary, share what felt okay for us and what didn't. That if we showed our authentic vulnerable selves, we would be punished, or ridiculed, or compared with others, or neglected, forgotten, laughed at, abandoned. We were taught to confuse our vulnerability with weakness, and see our sensitivity as something to be ashamed of.

Hiding our true feelings, repressing our authentic selves and creating a conceptual 'me', an image, a *persona* (mask) or character to win love and approval, and becoming something we were not—this became a matter of necessity, survival. Yes, *in order to survive, in order to win love*, we brilliantly and creatively did all we could to push down, suppress, numb or destroy the unwanted, 'dangerous, threatening, unsafe' energies inside us, de-pressing our true selves and creating a role called "me" to please the world, to avoid punishment or ridicule or neglect, to win attention and praise, to keep our primary relationships intact. We became performers, doing anything we could to distract others from our 'dark' insides. We pretended to be strong when we felt weak, up when we felt down, confident when we felt scared, controlled and cautious when we only longed to express our silliness and spontaneity and creativity. To the extent that we suppressed our true selves, we were all de-pressed, split and traumatised by our childhoods.

We abandoned ourselves for love, in our innocence. And to this day we may still feel like there is *something wrong with us*, deep down. The 'unacceptable' and 'dark' and 'shameful' feelings, desires and longings still fester inside of us, deep in the unconscious, draining our life energy and spirit, making us feel tired, depressed, lethargic, anxious and disconnected from life and each other. Unfelt and suppressed energies can become destructive and wreak havoc on our immune systems, feeding all manner of diseases, mental and physical. We may simply feel "dead while alive", and not know why. We may turn to addictions and compulsive behaviours—alcohol, drugs, sex, internet, television, shopping, overthinking, overworking—in order to find temporary relief from ourselves.

As Jesus said in the Gospel of Thomas:

"If you do not bring forth what is within you, what you do not bring forth will destroy you."

He was perfectly describing the experience of trauma.

Jesus also said:

"If you bring forth what is within you, what you bring forth will save you."

Through this 'bringing forth', flushing our wounds with loving awareness, which is the essence of true meditation, even the deepest inner pain and trauma can be transmuted into medicine.

In the presence of a safe friend, or therapist, or in the presence of God, ourselves, the mountains, the vastness of the oceans, or even a loving animal friend, we can find the courage to let our persona 'break down', and reconnect with the unloved parts of ourselves, 'bringing forth' those split-off shadowy energies into the Light of Awareness. We can take the risk of feeling more uncomfortable, more afraid, more unloved and unworthy and angry and chaotic than ever. We can take the risk of seeing ourselves, and being seen in return. Losing the image. Coming out of hiding. The suppressed chaos, the mess, the 'victim' part of us, the lost child, can now come back into the present moment, and this time, instead of receiving shame and judgement and ridicule and attack, *that very same material receives love, and breath, and understanding, and welcoming, and attention, and curiosity.* All the life-giving power trapped inside these suppressed emotions can pour back into our bodies, all the creativity of the anger, the sorrow, the guilt, the fear and the joy can now energise us, inspire us, make us feel whole and powerful and alive again. The energies that previously threatened to destroy us—our anger, our fear, our grief, our deepest and strangest and most creative desires— can now become our greatest teachers, friends and guides, and sources of nourishment and inspiration.

As the re-integration of healing happens, we may no longer be able live up to the image of the "cool, calm, collected spiritual practitioner"! We may scream, shake, weep, sweat, speak new and surprising words, or fall to the floor in exhaustion or in gratitude. We may look messy and broken and wild and 'crazy'. We may feel and think things that seem 'not like us at all'. We may feel we are about to die, or go mad, or lose ourselves completely. People we imagined were our friends may run from our chaos, or shame it, or try to 'save' us (to save themselves from their own discomfort). Our external lives may fall apart. Relationships may break up. Old reference points may disappear. New friends, new family, new lovers may arrive to support us in our process, to stay present with us as we fall apart and fall together and fall in love with our wildness again. As we return to the Garden. As we discover who we truly are, day by day, baby step by baby step.

In the midst of the crisis of healing, in any moment, we can leave the story and return to simplicity, the ever-present field of meditation. We can feel our feet on the ground. We can breathe. We can let old and powerful energies move through us, like the ancient sky allowing a storm. We can begin, moment by moment, to *trust* the body and its mysteries. We can remember our Divine Capacity—how much life we can hold, painful and pleasurable, violent and gentle, positive and negative, sacred and profane. *All* thoughts and feelings have a home in us. *All* parts of our humanity are lovable, sacred, natural.

We can hold it *all*, from the greatest joy to the deepest despair. Like a mother holding her new-born. Like the Earth, like the ground, holding you now, as you read these very words in this very ordinary book, on this very ordinary day, in this miraculous Now, in this present scene of this precious, unique and unrepeatable life you have been given.

Right now, what can you see? What can you hear? What can you feel? *Pay attention, just for a moment.* Are you feeling peaceful? Tense? Tired? Expansive? *Don't think. Look.* Is there a sense of struggle in you? Anticipation? Do you feel empty? Full? Is there an excitement, a sadness, a sense of loneliness, anxiety, joy? Is your mind calm or busy? What's it like to sit on this chair, to lie on this bed, to stand where you stand, to breathe as you breathe? Is your breathing fast or slow, shallow or deep?

Whatever is alive here, just for a moment, can you bless it with your undivided attention? Can you be here with this anxiety, without trying to fix it? Can you stay with this emptiness, without trying to fill it? Can you flush this loneliness, this joy, this doubt with non-judgemental attention? Can you behold this present moment as an artist would behold his subject, as a lover would behold her beloved? Not as something to change or mend, but as something whole and fascinating in itself? And if you can't be here, if you can't find a place of allowing, can you be with *that* feeling—of restlessness or resistance or frustration or refusal—just for a moment, without trying to fix it, or heal it, or transcend it, or make it go away...?

3. FROM DEPRESSED TO DEEP REST

Every human being on this planet, however happy they seem on the outside, is to some extent depressed, pressed down ('de-pressed') by the false self, exhausted on a deep soul level by their frustrated attempts to hold up an image, to play a character that isn't really who they are.

We simply long to stop performing and be authentic again. We long to wake up from the performance of separation, take off our costumes and make-up and tear up the script forced upon us by our family and our culture and simply *be*. When we repress our *true* feelings, desires, urges, longings, banishing them into the unconscious, living as a mask in this world, playing a cartoon version of ourselves, we become depressed, lethargic, numb and even suicidal.

The experience of *depression* is not a mistake, then, but deeply intelligent. It is a wake-up call. Depression is an ancient, yet highly misunderstood, invitation back to deep rest, slowness, presence, truth. It is a call to come out of the mind and its fears and anxieties and resentments, and back into the living body and its senses and its spontaneity. *It is a call to 'kill' the false self, the character we've been playing and be exactly what we are.* To let go of the image. To stop running from the living moment. To touch into our wounds and traumas with great gentleness. To mindfully drench our intimate, first-hand experience with loving attention. To awaken to our brilliant rage, our awesome grief and our astonishing hidden terrors. To walk our path, to forge ahead with courage. To speak our unique truth out loud. To stop de-pressing the wildness and creativity inside. To come out of hiding and allow ourselves to be seen. To die to the false, and awaken to the real.

My suicidal depression and existential despair ended up saving my life a hundred times over, pushing me onto this healing path. Depression was my unique call to discover the deepest kind of cosmic rest within myself. I am eternally grateful to the gods of the Underworld for making me so miserable that I started to question who I'd taken myself to be, and started to fall in love with the ground upon which I stood.

I did not need to destroy my body or kill my mind. I needed to kill my image of 'self', to stop confusing a picture of 'me' with who I really was. I needed to commit the compassionate spiritual 'suicide' of *falling in love with the present moment*. This is the great paradox of awakening. We must 'die' in order to really live. We must 'kill' (let go of) everything we are not, in order to flourish as who we really are. We must die to the false notion that we are not One with the stars, the moon, the migrating swallows at daybreak, the wild lavender and heather and rose of the mountains.

4. STOP WAITING FOR ABUNDANCE ⋙

When you were young, you loved to dream and let go of dreams. You dwelled in the Now.

As you got older, you started to take your dreams, end-points and goals way too seriously, and your happiness became bound up with the future, and destinations became more important than the journey itself.

You simply forgot how precious it was to be alive, each and every moment.

Dream about what you want, of course. Have a vision for an extraordinary future, of course. *But learn to let your dreams go, too,* let them float off into the river of life, and then bring your attention back to the place where all dreams begin and end, are born and die: the present moment. Don't use a dream or a hope as an excuse to disconnect from where you are, because where you are is way too valuable.

Learn to love the place where you are. Lean into the in-between moments. Embrace the ordinary steps on the path. The moments of 'nothing'. The seemingly inconsequential instants of life. The uneventful moments, the ones where nothing seems to be happening at all. Learn to love that nothing, the delicious sense of waiting, yearning, longing, seeking and anticipating 'the next thing'. Learn to dance and breathe in the space between the wanting and the getting, the dreaming and the fulfilment of dreams. *Learn to love not having what you want right now*. Learn to appreciate the movie scenes in-between the dramatic ones. The tremendous sense of potential there, the beauty and fullness of the space, the delicious sense of absence, the pregnant and fertile void, the *something* of the nothing.

Realise that 'lack' is only space, resisted. And even an 'incomplete' feeling, a feeling of emptiness, is so complete, a welcome visitor in the heart. Breathe into the belly, the chest, the tired head. Drench a sense of 'lack' with curious awareness. Infuse the body and its heaviness with light, saturate it with attention, fill it with love. Feel the weight and fullness of the torso, the shoulders, the neck, the legs, the entire body, abundant with sensation and the stillness between sensation.

Even when you don't have what you want, you are invited to want to be exactly where you are; to fall in love with the place where you stand or sit, to want it; to contact the fertile ground as you wait, or forget the waiting and simply savour the unique and unrepeatable moments in the mysterious movie called "You".

Open your arms in gratitude, ready to receive whatever comes, ready to bless whatever leaves, this is the calling of true meditation.

Because sometimes, even the 'not getting' can be so very *full*.

Behold, your abundant life!

"Please, don't try to fix me. I am not broken. I have not asked for your solutions.

When you try to fix me, you unintentionally activate deep feelings of unworthiness, shame, failure, even suicidal self-doubt within me. I can't help it. I feel like I have to change to please you, transform myself just to take away your anxiety, mend myself to end your resistance to the way I am. And I know I can't do that, not on your urgent timeline anyway. You put me in an impossible bind when you try to fix me. I feel so powerless.

I know your intentions are loving! I know you really want to help. You want to serve. You want to take away people's pain when you see it. You want to uplift, awaken, caretake, educate, inspire. You truly believe that you are a positive, compassionate, unselfish, nice, good, kind, pure, spiritual person. But I want you to know, honestly, friend, I actually feel deeply *unloved* when you try to 'love' me in this old way. It feels like you're trying to relieve your own tension when you attempt to fix me. I feel treated like a broken object that needs mending.

Under the guise of you being 'kind' and 'helpful' and 'spiritual', I feel suffocated, smothered, rejected, shamed, and completely unloved when you try to fix me. I feel abandoned in your love. Do you get that? I feel like you don't actually care about *me*, even though on the surface it sure looks like you care. But deep down it feels like you are holding an *image* of how I should be. *Your image. Not mine.* It looks like your love but it feels like your violence. Do you understand?

As soon as you stop trying to 'help' me, you are of the greatest help to me! I stop trying to change to please you! I feel safe, respected, seen, honoured for what I am. I can fall back into my own subjective power. I can trust myself again, the way you are trusting me. I can relax deeply.

Without your pressure, your demand for me to abandon myself and be different, healed, transformed, enlightened, awakened, mended, 'better', I can better see myself. I can discover my own inner resources. I can touch my own powerful presence. I feel safe enough to allow and express my true feelings, thoughts, desires, hold my own perceptions. I no longer feel smothered, a victim, a little child to your expert adult. The courageous warrior in me rises. I breathe more deeply. I feel my feet on the ground. Loving attention drenches my experience, even the uncomfortable parts. My senses feel less dull. Healing energies emerge from deep within. I feel light, free, liberated from your disapproval. I feel respected, not shamed. Seen as a living thing, not able to be compared with an image.

You help me so much when you stop trying to help me, friend! I need my *own* answers, my *own* truth, not yours. I want a friend, present and real, someone to hold me as I break and heal, not an expert or a saviour or someone trying to stop me going through my process.

And do you see, when you are trying to save me, you are actually abandoning yourself? You are running from your own discomfort, your own unlived potential, and focussing on mine? I become your ultimate distraction. I don't want to be that for you anymore..."

Let's stop trying to fix or save each other. Let's love each other instead. Bow to each other. Bless each other. Hold each other. As we are. As we actually, actually, actually are.

6. IF YOU ARE FEELING SAD...

If you are feeling sad, you are not in a 'low vibration'. You are not sick or broken or unenlightened or far from healing. You are not 'trapped in your ego' or stuck in the 'separate self'. You are not being negative, and you don't need to be fixed, and sadness is not a mistake, because it's life moving in you, and life can't be a mistake, ever.

You are just feeling sad, that's all.

It's a feeling state playing out on the vibrantly alive movie screen of presence, that's all.

It's not a problem that requires a solution or a Band-Aid. It's a sacred and precious part of you longing for love, acceptance, embrace, rest.

You've been blessed by sadness today; you've been chosen as her home; don't run away from such a truly precious visitor.

7. RELAX, YOU ARE NOT THE DOER

What is stress? Stress is the tension between this moment and your mental image of how this moment *should* be. Stress is your narrow focus on a mental list of 'future things to do', the imaginary pressure of 'all the things that haven't been done yet', 'all the other things I should be doing now', 'all the wonderful things I'm missing out on'.

Stress always involves past-and-future-thinking, a forgetting of your true Ground and your only place of power: This moment, here, now, today.

When your focus shifts from what is *not* present, to what *is* present, from 'lack' to what is abundantly here; when, instead of trying to complete a list of ten thousand things, you simply do the *next* thing, the *one* thing that presents itself now, *this thing here*, with your full attention and passion and presence, lists get completed effortlessly, and in some deeper sense, tasks do themselves.

Relax. You are not the doer.

8. THE RUPTURE AND THE REPAIR ⟿

When our plans and dreams fall apart, what doesn't fall apart?

First there is the rupture. The status quo is shattered. The old safety is gone. Old wounds are triggered, the pain body resurfaces, buried trauma erupts from the depths of the unconscious. You feel disoriented, groundless, homeless, not knowing where to turn. An old world has crumbled, a new world has not yet formed.

You encounter the strange space of Now, pure presence, raw, unprotected by old dreams, nothing to cling to. Even your outdated concepts of God crumble here.

And then you remember to breathe.

And you return to the safety of the present moment, and you feel your feet on the ground again, and you feel the weight of the body again, and you *observe* the madness of the mind rather than losing yourself in it. You watch your thoughts spinning out of control, but you, as awareness, are not spinning out of control with them. The world may feel out of control but you are not. **You are not the ever-changing mind, but the unchanging observer of it, and this realisation changes everything**

And you feel what you feel now. Afraid. Angry.

Numb. Sad. Lonely. Unsafe. Whatever. You commit to feeling it fully today, to not running away. A feeling is just a feeling, a flowing energy and not a solid fact, and presence can hold it as it flows. You wail, you weep, you scream, but you are repairing. You have broken to heal, ruptured to mend. Old energies have emerged only to be blessed with love, acceptance, tenderness, today; and there is only today.

You only ever have to deal with life a moment at a time. Please do not forget this.

You can't go back to the way things were. You can't un-see what you have seen. But you can be present, right now. And you can take each step consciously now, not automatically, habitually, but mindfully, with care. Finding gratitude for each extra moment you are alive. Thanking the air, the rain, the vastness of the sky. Thanking the feet and the legs and the spine as they keep you standing. Thanking the arms for all they hold and carry. Thanking the heart for what it endures, day by day. Thanking the shoulders, the brain, the lungs, the muscles, all the internal organs, full of unspeakable mysteries.

Staying close to yourself now, as your old world falls apart, walking this new and unknown path with trust and courage, slowly, mindfully, with care. Stepping into your new life, one step at a time, repairing your world with each step, becoming familiar with the moments.

"I can't live without you".

"You complete me".

"Without you, I'm nothing".

"Never leave me".

They sold you a beautiful lie about love. Nobody is coming to save you, you see. No prince on horseback. No Juliet. No "One Special Person". No surrogate mother. No messiah, no saviour, no God who will take away all your doubts, your pain, your feelings of emptiness, that sense of separation and abandonment that's been lodged in your guts since you were young. Nobody will be able to feel and integrate and metabolise your feelings for you. Nobody can do living and dying for you. Nobody has the power to permanently distract you from your inner journey. Nobody can own you or be owned by you. Nobody can complete you. Nobody is coming to save you. This is terrible, wonderful news.

Your other half, your completion, your salvation, your ultimate purpose in this life, is not outside of you, you see, but *deep within you*. It lives as your very own warm presence, burns like the Sun within.

So many people are looking for love, or they are trying to hold onto a love that seems to be slipping through their fingers. Or they feel they have lost love, and they are trying to get love back, running from uncomfortable feelings of withdrawal, numbing themselves with more dreams, running further and further from themselves, in pursuit of something they will never reach, still dreaming of that "One Special Person" who will complete them, provide them with a lifetime of psychological security, be the perfect mother or father they never had on Earth.

Of course, that's not love. That's fear, an urgent flight from aloneness.

We just never learned how to be alone.

If you can find or lose it, if you can be 'in' it or 'out' of it, if it can be given to you or taken away, if you have to fight for it, beg for it, manipulate yourself or others to get it, if you feel you have to become worthy of it, deserve it, win it, hold onto it, even *understand* it, then it's the mind's version of love. It is the lie, not the reality.

If you love, you are present. That's it. Love is simple and kind and effortless. If you love someone, you are present with them. As present with them as you are with yourself. As present as the Sun in the sky, despite the clouds, the storms, the ever-changing weather.

Do not confuse love with desire, then. Desire comes and goes. It burns brightly, or the flame extinguishes. But desire is not consistent, like love

Do not confuse love with attraction. Attraction is

beautiful, but it ebbs and flows, rises and falls like the ocean waves. It changes with the seasons, days, hours, moments. It is not ever-present, like love.

Do not confuse love with warm, pleasant feelings, chemical feelings, limerent feelings of being "in love". Pleasurable feelings turn to painful ones so quickly. Love is not pleasure nor pain, it is not ecstasy nor hurt; it is the field that endures, even as the bliss fades into despair. It is the space for *all* feelings.

Do not confuse love with the urgency to possess someone or be possessed. Love is not infatuation. Love is not obsessive nor compulsive. Love does not cling. Love does not own anything; it is weightless, transparent, formless and clear. Love does not say "I need you for my happiness, my contentment, my life". No, love is synonymous with freedom, with a wide open heart, with the willingness to feel every feeling, think every thought.

The most dangerous myth is the one that tells us that another person has the power to 'make us happy'. No, no. Happiness, true happiness, the kind of happiness that cannot be bought or sold or neatly packaged, is identical with your own presence, which nobody can give to you, and nobody can take away. It is ageless and timeless and formless, yet as solid and real as *the experience of reading these words now.*

If you look to another for happiness, you will always depend on them, always be afraid of losing them, and anxiety and resentment will rumble underneath your 'love'. You will adapt yourself to please them, numb your most uncomfortable thoughts and feelings, close your eyes to the truth and live in fantasy and hope. You will make yourself unhappy in order to win their love, keep them, make them stay interested. You will make yourself unhappy trying to make them happy... or forcing yourself to be happy instead. That is not love, it is an addiction, addiction to a person and an idea. It is fear masquerading as 'romance'. It is the lie.

But underneath every addiction is the longing for home, for Mother in the deepest sense of the word.

Find the deepest sense of home within yourself, then. Make your body your home and your mother, your breath your father, your belly your dearest friend as it rises and falls in the present moment, your hands, your shoulders, the way your face feels, the weight of your clothes and the sounds of the morning, afternoon, evening, night, make them all your lovers. Find your ground in the sense of being alive, in the look in the eyes of a friend, in the sounds of the morning traffic and the smell of freshly baked bread, in the yearning and excitement and boredom that accompanies you each day. And in that place of presence, spend time with others who nourish you, who help you feel alive, who empathise with you and can validate your precious feelings. When you are not trying to win love, when you are not running from your own uncomfortable feelings, you can afford to truly love and be loved.

Invite others into your love field; let them stay,

let them leave, bow to their path and walk your own with courage. But do not for a moment buy into the lie that salvation lies anywhere except at the very heart of your exquisite presence, the place where there's nobody to be saved and nobody to do the saving. The place of true meditation. The place where you touch life, and are touched in return, moment by moment...

For you are The One, your own greatest lover, partner, friend, guru and Mother. And so you can say to yourself, every morning when you wake, and every night before you sleep, and upon every in-breath and out-breath:

"I can't live without myself".

"I complete myself, in every moment".

"Without myself, I'm nothing".

"Where I begin, life begins..."

10. THE SILENCE BETWEEN US

In some Native American cultures, it's considered polite to wait up to several minutes before responding to a question or taking one's turn in a conversation. Replying too soon is considered rude, because it shows that you obviously haven't truly *listened* to the other person.

Many of us in the modern world would find even a few moments of such silence in a conversation awkward, uncomfortable, even embarrassing. Sometimes we speak not because we have anything important or authentic or heartfelt to say, not because we even *want* to talk really, but because we feel we *have* to. We feel uncomfortable, nervous, anxious about *not talking*. We speak in order to avoid the void, silence the silence, distract from the extraordinary absence at the heart of life. We speak in order to run from ourselves and each other.

Slow down, friend. Get out of your head and into your body. Take a few moments to just feel your feelings in a conversation. Let yourself feel awkward and uncomfortable, vulnerable and a little shaky in the silence if you must. It's *just a feeling*, it won't hurt you, you can bear it, and the silence will hold it anyway. Take the risk of the other person sensing your feelings of awkwardness, or thinking that you're boring or strange or have nothing to say. Hey, at least you are real! At least you aren't hiding behind a wall of words. At least you are trying to connect in a deeper way. At least you have the courage to feel awkward and not distract yourself from that, *not abandon yourself when you need yourself the most.*

Bring some space into your conversations today. Listen. Wait. Listen some more. Lean into the awkwardness. Respond from the heart, not the mind and its fears. Let your conversations breathe a little. Know that the other person is probably feeling as awkward and unprepared as you are, deep down.

Our deepest connections are always made in silence. Witness a mother rocking her baby to sleep, two old friends or lovers passing time in a café, or a simple silent walk in nature, just you and the forest at dawn. Words are not necessary for us to feel each other, know each other, understand life and each other very deeply indeed.

Maybe, with all our clever words, we're all just trying to find our own sweet way back to that exquisite silence, the silence we came from, the silence to which we shall all return.

11. THE BEST SELF-HELP ADVICE ⌇

There is no self to help. The best self-help advice of all.

When you try to 'help' the 'self' you reinforce an illusion: That there is a broken self today, an incomplete self that is 'less than' a future self.

And you strengthen identification with a mind-made entity called 'me'. An image. A mirage.

You forget your nature as Presence itself.

When you give up trying to help a self, you sink into an unconditional embrace: The embrace that is Life Itself. Where all your imperfections, your doubts, sorrows, joys and fears, your longings and your ecstasies, even your imagination of 'self', and your frustrated attempts to 'fix' it, or 'help' it reach a future perfection, are 100% embraced. Already.

No self to save. No self to fix. No self to enlighten. No self to lose. No self to transcend. Just an exquisite moment. An unlimited divine perfection, shimmering through this human imperfection. Shining through the self-help, its success and its failure too, its longing and its frustration, its exhaustion and its surrender.

So help yourself, friend, by ending the exhausting search for a better self... and simply relaxing into this unique Now.

12. ON BEAUTY

Beauty isn't there in *what* you see. It's there in *how* you see.

There is a vast field of loving possibility where your presence meets the presence of the 'other'.

Yet there are not two presences, only one, just as fire never truly divides.

Beauty is not contained, see, but spills out through every crack and crevice in reality, gushing like an unstoppable river.

There are no others here; you are only meeting yourself.

See beautifully, then, see through the innocent eyes of awareness, and the world around you is suddenly beautiful. Your seeing changes everything. And leaves everything perfectly unchanged.

13. EVEN WHEN WE CANNOT HOLD OURSELVES 〰️

I was speaking with a young man about letting go of his ideas about the future, his images of how his life 'should' be, and embracing himself as he actually was, *feeling* his pain instead of running from it, living in the present, not in false hope.

He said, "Well Jeff, if there's only this moment, only *now*, and that's all there is… then I'm going to kill myself".

For a moment, he had lost all hope. Suicide seemed like the logical solution.

I stayed present. Listened. Validated his pain. Entered his world.

Discovering presence can be a shock to the system, can begin to reorganise the entire psyche, release deeply buried feelings, urges, longings, fears. I understand that. I've been through it.

"Yes, it is *scary* to lose all your hope."

"I'm terrified."

"Where is that fear? Can you describe it to me? Can you feel it in your body now?"

"Yes. It's burning… Fiery… Here… in my chest."

"Would you be willing to stay right there for a moment, feel that power in your chest?"

Silence.

"It's hot… and I feel like… I feel like I want to *kill* someone. You know, I feel so *pissed* at you now. You've taken away everything from me, all my hope…"

I stayed present.

"I understand. Yes. So where do you *feel* that anger?"

"Here, in my belly, my throat, my chest…"

"What does it feel like, again?"

"It's like… Power. Like a volcano. Like… I could destroy the whole Universe."

"Yes. Yes. It's huge. You're feeling your own power. You don't have to deny it any more, or act on it, just feel it now, for a moment here; let's let it burn, honour it together".

"Wow. It's a lot."

"It's yours. Just allow it. Allow those sensations in your belly, heart, throat. Breathe into them, through them…"

"I want to scream."

"Do it!"

"I…. I…. I hate life!"

"Louder!"

"I HATE LIFE! I HATE EVERYONE! I HATE

MY PARENTS!"

"Yes! What else do you hate?"

"I HATE *YOU*, JEFF!"

Our eyes meet. A recognition. Love. Presence. *Total acceptance.*

He bursts into tears, slumps in his chair, his body relaxes, he breathes deeply again.

His grief and rage had been met, for the first time ever I think, with love, understanding, acceptance. Something had been released, some tension, some trauma, something bound-up, something old. Something seemingly unlovable had been loved for the first time. Some new neural pathway had been forged. Something unconscious had come into conscious awareness, this open meditative space, and received kind attention and blessings. *The seeker had received what it had always been seeking.*

"My God. My God. For the first time in my life, Jeff, honestly, for the first time, I feel... *alive*. I feel like... *myself*."

It's amazing, the power of *just staying present*. Listening to what emerges. Doing less and trusting more. Allowing the other person to *go through what they have to go through*, without trying to fix or save them. Making it safe for them to be fully themselves, fully alive and fully messy, to express what they have to express, to feel as bad or as good as they need to feel.

Through the hate, to the love. Through the grief, to the joy. Taking away the false hope, and perhaps leaving them with the dawn of a new hope. Trusting their individual process. Trusting in their ability to withstand powerful thoughts and feelings. Trusting this vast field of meditation, the benevolent field that holds us all, always, even when we cannot hold ourselves.

14. THE GRACE OF DISAPPOINTMENT 🪶

If you run from disappointment, you run from life itself.

Disappointment can soften the mind and open the heart. If you let it.

Don't be afraid.

When our hopes, dreams and expectations shatter, it can hurt like hell. When life doesn't turn out the way we'd hoped, disappointment can burn hot inside. The invitation? *Turn towards the burning place.* Actually feel the pain, instead of numbing it or running towards some new dream. It's more painful to run away, in the end. The pain of self-abandonment is the worst pain of all.

Break the addiction to 'the next experience'. Bring curious attention to that which you call 'disappointment'. Contact the fluttery sensations in the belly, the constricted feeling in the heart area, the lump in the throat, the fogginess in the head. Stay present with what's alive. Be with what's screaming for attention. Do not refuse the Now.

Turn towards this burning moment; this is true meditation. Breathe into the uncomfortable place. Don't abandon yourself now for a new imagined future. Don't leave yourself for the world of thought. Find your home in *what is*.

Let the mind chatter away today, but don't take it as reality. Disappointment is bringing you closer to yourself. To your breath. To the weight of your body upon the Earth. To the sounds of the afternoon. To the evening's song. To the sense of being alive. To a deep surrender to the imperfection of this human experience.

You've been lost in your head, friend. Return to your heart now. Soften into the moment. Weep out the old dreams. Return Home.

This moment is as it is. This moment as it is.

Let all expectations melt. Into silence. Into a new beginning.

Disappointment is the gateway.

15. I BREATHE WITH YOU

Do not look for love; do not wait for it; do not expect it on-demand. You will always feel incomplete, and the fear of 'loss of love' will rumble under your days.

Love is not a subscription service. Love is not a reward for good behaviour. Love is not something you 'deserve' or do not. It is your birthright; so find it within your own heart.

When you notice attention going outwards, when you notice the mind seeking, striving, manipulating, trying to understand, clinging, holding, *stop*. Invite attention closer. Thank the mind for its hard work, and move attention to the sensations of your feet on the ground, the feel of the weight of your body as it is pulled towards the Earth. To the breath, so dependable, so ancient, rising and falling, rising and falling, like a wave in the vastness of your being.

Invite attention to wash down through the throat, the chest, into the pit of the stomach; let it infiltrate the raw, tingly, fluttery, flickering, dynamically alive sensations there. Let attention drench your sorrow, your loneliness, that sense of abandonment you've been running from, pretending it wasn't really there. For a moment, provide a sanctuary for these ancient ones, these beautiful fragments of a great puzzle you started long ago, before the Big Bang, before time itself. Let this present scene of the movie of your life be sanctified with attention, with this kindly awareness called love. This is prayer.

I am here. I am here. And it's okay. Even though it doesn't feel okay, it's okay. My sadness is intelligent. My fear is ancient, and sacred, and worthy. My longing burns with life. Even my doubts are my kin. Nothing is wrong here; all is held in love.

Life is so short, yet love is infinite, and bountiful, and ever-present, and closer than the next breath. So do not look for love; do not wait for it; do not expect it on-demand. But know it. Know its presence, the intimacy of it. Feel it whispering in your ear...

I breathe with you, my love. Every inhale, every exhale, and the spaces in-between. When you are on your knees, exhausted by life's chaos and uncertainty, I kneel with you. When you are exalted, held up high by this fickle world, I rejoice with you. When you feel lost, and you cannot go on, I have already found you. Here. Here, always here. I am so very near. I laugh with you, cry with you, bleed with you; your blood is mine. Your voice is my voice, your silence my silence, and I would go to the ends of the Earth to find you, to fight for you, to bring you home.

You cannot escape love; that is why you cannot grasp it.

And so if I had a prayer, it would already be answered; the prayer and the resolution as One; the gift given long ago.

16. THE BEAUTY OF YOUR NUMBNESS

Many people share with me that they feel numb, disconnected, stuck, blocked, frozen, dissociated. Like they cannot feel anything at all.

They have been to every therapist, tried every pill, been treated like an object and come to see themselves as a broken thing that cannot be fixed. They are exhausted from the fight. They long to be free from their numbness.

I remind them: it's a miracle that they can feel numb at all. It's amazing how in touch with their numbness they are, how sensitive to the disconnection within. What a blessing. Most people in the world are so distracted, so preoccupied with past and future, so disconnected from their bodies that they aren't *aware* of their numbness at all.

Being *aware* of your disconnection, your dissociation, your alienation from feeling, is a massive step on the pathless path of healing. Ironically, you have to be very sensitive, awake and alive, to actually *notice* your numbness in the first place.

"I'm numb" is, on closer inspection, a story, a narrative, an interpretation by thought, a photograph in the mind, and not the actual reality. Come closer to the body. Where is the numbness in your body, right now (and there is only now)? Are there some parts that feel more numb than others? Notice that there must be areas that feel more alive for other areas to feel numb by contrast. Bring the warmth of your loving and curious attention to a 'numb' place. Now, drop the word 'numb' (it's a very loaded, judgemental label) and directly feel the raw physical sensations— or lack of sensations—there, moment by moment, without trying to 'feel less numb'. Dignify this area with curiosity and breath and the warmth of your loving attention. Go slow. Be patient. Bless whatever you find, and bless whatever you don't find.

Perhaps a 'numb' place is just a place that longs for your love, your curiosity, your non-judgemental presence. Perhaps it is a place in the body that's starved of attention and oxygen. Instead of trying to fix it, to make it 'come alive', can you slow down, and actually infuse it with your awareness? So you are *no longer numb to your numbness*, no longer disconnected from your disconnection, no longer dissociated from your dissociation. This is a massive step.

In the warmth of the sun's love, even the iciest of places can thaw. The way out of numbness is through.

And remember, if you are connected with your numbness, if you are aware of the empty place inside of you, if you can begin to lean into it, make room for it, give it attention, and breath, and compassion, and your precious time, *you are not numb at all.*

17. WHY YOU HAVEN'T HEALED YET

Are you wondering why, after all these years, you haven't healed, awakened, transformed? Why your pain, confusion, doubts, sorrows, your deep longings and yearnings for home, are *still here*? Why, *by now*, your pain has not gone?

"I should have found the answers by now. By now, my sorrow should have disappeared. By now, I should be free from shame and fear. By now, I should be feeling more peaceful, clear, relaxed, awakened. By now, joy should be permanent, my natural state. By now I should be finished with suffering, done with doubt. By now I should be healed. What is wrong with me?"

Friend, *by now* is the biggest lie of all! There is no such thing as *by now*. There cannot be a *by now*.

Think about it. There is only Now. Only this moment. No *by*.

Instead of clinging to ideas of how we should be *by now*, can we instead bow to what is actually here, honour our present experience, see its sacredness and its intelligence, celebrate *the way we are today*, even if we feel sad, even if we experience doubt, or anger, or fear, or loneliness? Then, we may experience a total paradigm shift...

From:

"Pain, sadness, anger, fear, why are you still here? I wanted you to be gone by now!"

To:

"Ohhh! You are here! Yes! What an honour to meet you, here! You are life, too; a sacred wave of consciousness! There is no mind-made story that says you shouldn't be here! No demand for you to have disappeared 'by now'! You are not 'still' here, of course; there is no time. You are here, now, in this moment, only! Still here! I am still here, and we can be still, here! And in the stillness, in this oceanic field of Presence, we can truly meet..."

A thought or feeling does not arise to be healed, friend; it arises to be held, lightly, in the loving arms of present awareness.

The bad news is that you will never get *there*. And that's also the best news of all. For you are *here*, always. You are always, already here. You will always be here, because here *is* there. Here is your home and your sanctuary. This is true healing: the surrender into Presence, the sense of being held by something infinitely greater than yourself. No time required.

This is the great paradox of healing:

You are always healing (in time)

and

you are already healed (in the timelessness of Now).

When a friend feels 'done' with this life, when their world no longer makes sense, your simple listening can be the greatest medicine of all.

Cry with them. Wonder with them. Be silent with them. Be certain or uncertain with them. Witness them as they are today. Look into their eyes. Tell them you love them, and you would love for them to stay around. Validate their feelings, however painful. Help them feel acknowledged in this world. Saturate their experience with listening.

They are going through a crisis of identity; this is not the end, this is not the final scene, only a cry for support, a heart dialling another heart. Don't offer clever answers now. Offer yourself. Don't preach and teach and sermonise. Don't judge them, or make them feel wrong for thinking their thoughts or desiring what they desire. Embrace them. So they do not feel alone. So they can touch upon their own courage. Their capacity to withstand painful feelings and go on. As the sky withstands the fiercest storms, and goes on.

When a friend feels 'done' with this life, when their world no longer makes sense, love them even more! Bow to their honesty, their courage in telling the truth; and celebrate the vast intelligence in them that's finally 'done' with all the pretending and the lies. Fierce patience is required here: a new friend is being born; the old one was too small. It's painful and scary to shed skin, but it's ultimately more painful to live in old skin.

The ground is sacred now because you are present with your friend as they touch into their sacred depths and cry out to the gods, "I am done with this life!"

Hopelessness is a crucible; there is always new hope in Presence.

19. WE ALL HAVE TENDER PLACES

It's easy to say "I love you". It's easy to talk about love, and presence, and awareness, and a deep acceptance of what is. It's easy to teach, to say things that sound true, and good, and spiritual.

But they are just words. There is a world before words.

When anger surges, as it will, can you stay close, and not numb it, or lash out? When fear bursts in the body, can you breathe into it, and not fuse with it, or run away into stories, but stay right in the middle? When you feel hurt, rejected, unloved, abandoned, can you make room for that feeling, welcome it in the body, bow to its intensity, its fire, its presence, and not attack, or act out, or call people names? Can you commit to not abandoning yourself now that you need your own love the most?

It's easy to talk about love. It's easy to teach and preach. Until our old wounds are opened. Until life doesn't go our way. What triggers you is inviting you to a deeper self-love. Can you see?

There is no shame in this: *We all have tender places.*

20. RELATIONSHIP YOGA 🙢

The healthiest relationships are the honest ones, the ones grounded in Presence, not fantasy, false promises or unconscious hope. Where two souls can share their authentic, real-time, embodied selves with each other, reveal their deepest truths—raw, messy, unresolved, unfinished and rough at the edges—and continually let go of their preconceived, conditioned ideas about how they 'should' be. The relationship is continually renewed in the crucible of intimacy. There may be ruptures, misunderstandings, intense feelings of doubt, anger, fear, anxiety and groundlessness along the way, yes, of course, but there is a mutual willingness to face this mess as it arises. To be vulnerable. To say "I hurt, I am in pain", and not blame the other for that pain. To say "I need some support" but not demand it of the other. To share desires and hopes and longings and dreams and not command that the other should see things in the same way. To receive their 'no' and their 'yes' too, even if it hurts. To stay in the crucible of transformation; to look with wide open eyes together at the present rupture, not turning away, or clinging to 'the way it used to be' or following other people's ideas about how things 'should' be. To let second-hand concepts of happiness burn up. To sit together sometimes in the rubble of shattered dreams and expectations, plans and hopes, and work towards finding a place of reconnection, repair and reconstruction. This is the courageous and often intense work of relationship.

To connect, even if we have to begin by admitting present feelings of disconnection. This is a relationship that is alive. A relationship that makes space for our deepest longings, fears, pains, yet does not expect the other to resolve these, to fix us or to take the hurt away. A relationship that asks the other to be a witness and a midwife for our own healing. And offers that same gift in return.

To inspire each other to find our own happiness. Even if that means letting go of or 'breaking up' the relationship in its current form. Love holds the other lightly, it does not cling or attempt to control. It only wants the best for the other, only wants them to step into their power, live their fullest life, find their deepest joy, follow their original path, learn to love their bodies and their own deepest feelings and desires, and find new ways to take care of themselves.

'I love you, and I want you to flourish.'

Relationship can be the ultimate yoga, yes, an ever-deepening adventure and rediscovery of ourselves and each other, rediscovering ourselves in the mirror of each other, a continual letting-go and a meeting, a dance of aloneness and togetherness, not losing ourselves in either extreme but resting and playing somewhere in the middle. Sometimes coming together, sometimes moving apart. Closeness and space. Intimacy with other, intimacy with self. Breathing in, breathing out. Morning and evening. Birth, and death.

Relationship is not a place we reach, a point of arrival, a destination; it is alive, and forever a point of departure, a beginning, each day. We can only start together, here, and there is joy in that beginning. There is excitement in the not knowing. There is life in the continual death of expectations. Staying close to a healthy fear of loss. Staying near to the groundlessness of things without losing ourselves in that groundlessness. Finding safety in the uncertainty. Breathing in, and breathing out.

As Eckhart Tolle says, relationships aren't here to make us happy—for true and lasting Happiness lies within us all, as that unshakable Presence that nobody can ultimately give us, or take away. We are safe either way. Others will not complete us. They will not save us, or resolve our deepest inner turmoil for us. They will, however, give us the gift of exposing our wounds, our inner children, those lost fragments, bringing them to the surface, exposing the places that are crying out for empathy, those beautiful orphans of light.

And then, a risk! To reveal our raw hearts, our loneliness, our vulnerability, our sensitivity, our not knowing, our joy, our 'shameful' secrets, to another human being on this small blue planet in the vastness of space. To drop the mask and expose the unprotected, unguarded heart. To risk being rejected, left alone, shamed and ridiculed. To risk a repetition of the old, perhaps.

But a bigger 'risk', maybe: To be loved for who we are! To be held in the blinding light of another's fascinated attention, like a baby held with such tenderness by an adoring, attentive father or mother. To be met in the present moment, nowhere to hide, nowhere to run. To let in the New. To risk losing the image, the false self, the carefully constructed persona, and to let another embrace the softness here. This is the highest possibility of relationship. *To see another's exquisitely delicate heart and to let your own soft heart be seen.* In the seeing, there can be healing, transformation, great beauty. We can be therapeutic vessels for our brothers and sisters. We can bring each other medicine, encouragement and great companionship on this sometimes lonely path of coming alive before we die.

And maybe it takes a lifetime to discover: The One you always longed for was actually deep inside of you from the beginning. And to have that One reflected by another—a partner, a friend, a lover, a therapist, or an animal, a tree, a mountain, the moon or the Vastness of the Cosmos—even if it's only for a moment...

...well, then you will know heaven on earth.

21. WHEN WE PUSH FEELINGS AWAY

In meditation, when a wave of feeling comes to visit —a grief, a fear, an unexpected anger or melancholy —can you stay present with that wave, breathe into it, let go of trying to 'let go' of it, and simply let it be, let it live, let it express itself right now within you? Can you notice the impulse in you to resist it, refuse it, distract yourself from it and move away from your experience? Don't judge or shame yourself for that impulse either, for wanting to have a different experience than you're having—it's an old habit, this urge to disconnect, this impulse to flee, this addiction to 'elsewhere'.

But see, today, if you can stay very close to 'what is', see if you can actually connect with the visiting feeling, gently lean in to your experience as it happens. Instead of shutting down, moving away, denying the energy in the body, can you gently open up to it? Can you flush it with curious attention? Let it move in you? Stay present throughout its life cycle, as it is born, expresses what it has to express, and falls back into Presence, its oceanic home?

All feelings are only looking for a home in you. Unfinished, stuck feelings, energies that have been resisted, pushed away, denied, banished, do not actually disappear. They live on in the darkness of the Unconscious, homeless and hungry for love, pulling the strings in our relationships, our bodies, our work in the world, getting in the way of our joy. Screaming for attention, deep down in the Underworld, they sap and drain our vitality and self-expression, cause us to become reactive, compulsive and obsessive, depressed and anxious, and ultimately affect our physical health... all in their attempts to get us to listen.

Until one day, deep in meditation, perhaps, we remember, all feelings are sacred and have a right to exist in us, even the messiest and most inconvenient and painful ones. And we remember to turn towards our feelings instead of running away. To soften into them. To make room for them instead of numbing them out or ignoring them.

The hungry ghosts, these lost children, now fed with our love, our warm attention, our curiosity and Presence, now given a holding environment within us, can finally come to rest. They no longer need to pull the strings in our lives. They now have the warmth and empathy they always longed for.

So much of our precious life force, our prana, our sacred energy, is spent on this Sisyphean task of pushing our feelings away, trying to make them go 'somewhere else'. But where would they go? There is only you. When you push them away, you only push them further into yourself.

So much creativity is released, so much relief is felt, when we break this age-old pattern of self-abandonment and repression, go beyond our fearful conditioning, and try something totally new: staying close to feelings, as they emerge in the freshness of the living moment, waving to us, calling to us, seeking their true home in our heart of hearts.

22. YOUR GREAT PROTECTOR

Spiritual teachings that tell us to extinguish our anger completely, that judge anger to be a categorically 'negative' and 'destructive' emotion, or call it 'unhealthy' or even 'unspiritual', can be very misleading teachings indeed.

Anger is life, a powerful expression of the vital life force that infuses and flows through and animates all things, and must be honoured as such.

Of course, we don't want to be ruled by our anger! We don't want anger to speak for us, put words in our mouths or control our bodies and behaviours. We want to have space around our anger, be able to use it consciously, as a tool, when necessary and appropriate and kind. We don't want to be consumed by it, identified with it, blocked by it, or lose ourselves to it. We want a healthy—and even loving—relationship with this most powerful and fiery of friends.

When we try to be 'spiritual' and suppress our anger, when we push it deep down into our bodies and into the waiting room of the unconscious, it festers there and wreaks havoc with our immune systems. We no longer 'have' anger. Anger 'has' us. Anger is no longer a feeling that comes and goes. We *are* angry now; anger is in our bones, we are identified with it. We find ourselves perhaps exploding in aggression and rage in our search for relief from the pressure within. Or maybe we become passive-aggressive, simmering quietly with resentment and hostility towards the world and others—the neighbours, politicians, family members, our partners. We find other unconscious ways to express or deflect from the anger: lying, blaming, sarcasm, complaining, or simply giving others 'the silent treatment'. All ways to avoid ourselves. We are still angry inside. Even if we think we are "spiritual" and "beyond anger". There are stories of the most "peaceful" and "enlightened" and "spiritually evolved" gurus and self-help teachers exploding with rage behind the scenes at students or shaming and blaming staff members or participants. The anger never really goes away, you see, it just finds new and creative ways to move.

There is a healthy, sacred middle between numbing our anger on the one hand, and habitually acting it out and hurting others on the other hand. Between *repression*, pushing the anger down, and unconscious, reactive *expression*, pushing the anger out in search of relief.

In the middle, which is the sacred realm of meditation, we can breathe, and we can begin to actually *feel* our anger deep inside our bodies. We can come out of our minds—out of the drama in the head, the blame and the attack on others and the revenge fantasies—and go right into our own bellies, chests, throats, solar plexus, head. Go right to the core of the aliveness, to the raw fiery sensations of the present moment. The intense, pulsating, throbbing, shuddering, fluttering, tickly, hot, fizzing sensations!

And we can inhale and exhale into them, bring our warm presence there, let them move in us, bless the wonderful uncontrollable mess of our bodies. We can drench 'the angry child' inside with the love he or she so desperately needs.

We can slow down and *respond* lovingly to our anger instead of unconsciously *reacting* to it.

From a place of presence, we can take responsibility for our anger instead of projecting it all over the place, instead of blaming, shaming and being unkind to others and making them responsible for how we feel. We can say "Yes, I feel angry!", honour the vibrant feeling that moves in us, see it as natural, healthy, holy —not a mistake or a failure of ours, or a sign that we are 'unevolved' or 'unspiritual'.

And underneath the anger, if we slow down, and breathe, and pay attention, we may simply find a vulnerable, fragile human heart. A sadness. A disappointment. An uncertainty. A tenderness that longs to be seen, embraced, welcomed. A sense of rejection. A feeling of being unheard. A need that is asking to be met.

Anger was the protection. Not a mistake, but a protection.

And we can thank anger for serving its purpose. For trying to keep us safe against the 'others'. For guarding our soft fleshy sensitive frightened heart. For trying to help us get our needs met. For trying to get others to listen.

Underneath the adult persona, see: an innocent child inside, calling, begging, screaming, raging for attention:

"Hear me. See me. Love me. Protect me. I am not a mistake..."

Follow the roar of anger to its vulnerable, spiritual core.

Fall in love with your great Protector.

23. STAND STRONG LIKE A ROCK!

Don't focus on what's 'wrong' with the world. When you fight against a broken world, when you live in resistance and inner violence, you contribute to the outer violence you see.

See the world as it is, the way an artist would look at a face, with all its flaws, imperfections, ridges, bumps, crevices and creases. See the light and the dark, the love and the flight from love, the kindness and its forgetting. See it all in fascination. Love the world now for how it appears. Hold the world in your loving arms. She is young, and making mistakes, and learning.

And from this place of love, re-enter the world. Stand strong like a rock, illuminating the world with your powerful presence. Speak up for those without a voice. Amplify messages of understanding and compassion. Spread the truth.

Fight *for* what you know and love, not *against* what you oppose and reject.

Your attention is your greatest blessing, so bless the world you are birthing now with your loving attention; do not energise a dying world with your intolerance.

Gather together with your brothers and sisters. Discover your true family, beyond colour, race, religion, belief. Unite in the name of love.

Now you are not attacking the world but fighting alongside her, and all her angels fight with you.

24. WHEN LOVE CRACKS YOU OPEN ✎

Love does not always feel safe because love is pure potential and pure presence and in pure presence every feeling and impulse is welcome, however gentle, however painful, however inconvenient, however fierce.

So when you let someone matter to you and you let yourself matter to someone and you are not ruled by fear your heart will have no choice but to crack to the hugeness of love and you will not be able to control the results and that's why the ego cannot love.

Safe, unsafe. Happy, sad. Certain, uncertain. Afraid, fearless. Fragile, powerful. Worthy, worthless, and everything in between. There is so much life now trying to fill you up, and you can barely contain it all. You are full of life, penetrated by life, pregnant with life.

They lied to you about love, you see, they said it was always supposed to feel good and warm and happy, they said it was something you'd be given, something you'd have to earn, or deserve, they said it was all butterflies and angels and light, but really it was always you, naked, raw and alive, cracked, whole, vulnerable, shaky but real, inhaling a cosmos, exhaling euphoria and the darkness and the grief and the joy of humanity and sometimes not knowing what the hell you're doing or how you're still alive.

Good. *Breathe.* All is unfolding beautifully, here. Love is not only gain, it is also loss. The beloveds will die and the loved ones will vanish, but love will not. She will simply make you rise, you see, and fall again, and wonder again if you will ever rise. She will open you and close you and break you and humble you and laugh at your childhood fantasies of love.

But it is all natural, and it is all *for* you. You will come full circle before long, back to yourself, the Origin. You were only ever seeking your own Heart, and its multitude of reflections.

Love is here. Love is always here. Somewhere between the euphoria and the darkness she found you. And the very ground you stand on is blessed, and you are safe once more.

So cry, laugh, shake, vomit, doubt the ground; you will never be abandoned by the Heart.

Everyone in your life is loving you right now, to the best of their ability. Their hearts are as closed or as open as they can possibly be right now, given their traumas, their beliefs, their willingness to look at themselves, the unbearable feelings they are repressing in their unconscious, the ways in which they are running from themselves.

Everyone is dealing with sorrows, fears and joys you may never know. Seeking love in their own way. Battling with monsters in the underworld you may never witness.

When you're trying to get love from others, it really matters how open or closed their hearts are today. You go to war with them, trying to crack them open, trying to unlock their love.

When you're not seeking love, but instead knowing love as your own true nature, feeling the source of love in your own brilliant heart, you are free, and the battle for love ends.

You can now let others love you in their own unique way. However 'limited' that may seem to the mind.

Because through the eyes of abundance, even limited love is a blessing. An open heart is a miracle, yes, but a closed heart is also to be honoured.

So you can let others love you as much as they are able to, today.

You are no longer a beggar for love.

For you know the true source of love. *You.*

There must be people who go mad or take their own lives because there is so much life inside of them and they feel unable to express it or even access it.

You are not *sick* if sexual urges towards man, woman or beast move through you. Let them move through. They won't control you when you *breathe through them*. No need to 'get rid' of them, and no need to act on them either in your search for relief. They are just pictures moving through the mind, images on the great movie screen of awareness, and the more you *allow* them, the less of a problem they are. Stop judging yourself, and no need to judge yourself for judging yourself. The mind is pure creativity, and we have little power to control our thoughts. Our power actually lies in our ability to *lovingly embrace* all that passes through the theatre of the mind, to make space for the mind's "sound and fury", to know that ultimately it all "signifies nothing".

Let the mind be the mind, and know that *you are not the mind*.

You are not *damaged* if thoughts of death come to visit. Bless them and let them pass, for they always pass and they are only thoughts, voices, vivid pictures.

You are not crazy if intense feelings of joy or sorrow, terror or rage surge through you unexpectedly, and sometimes all at the same time. Be the courageous space for these feelings, not their slave.

You are not *disturbed* if disturbing images play out on the movie screen of Awareness, because *you are the unchanging screen* and not the ever-changing pictures.

Make room in yourself for the light and the darkness, the weird and the strange and the erotic and the taboo and the unique and the inconvenient. Repress nothing and deny nothing and then none of it will control or frighten you. You will see: *all thoughts are your children too.*

Radical self-love is the deepest kind of joy there is; the permission to be wild, free, alive within.

And know there is nothing *wrong* with you, ever.

27. DEEP IN THE TANTRIC MUD

We have been sent gurus, guides, angels, healers, provocateurs, allies and antagonists in all shapes and sizes. Our partners, our kids, friends and family members, lovers. Our therapists, our work colleagues, strangers on the subway.

Our true teachers are all around us. Because the true teachings of life are ancient and lie deep within us.

All the people in our lives right now have gifts to offer. Some gifts are obvious. Some gifts are only realised in hindsight.

Through some relationships we are taught how to listen. To receive someone else's truth without rushing in to fix them, advise them or stop them feeling what they're feeling. To take their world seriously. To get out of our own heads. To lose our self-absorption and narcissism and step into different shoes.

Some relationships teach us how to hear ourselves, connect with our own wants and needs. To share our authentic feelings honestly, speak what's really going on in our inner world, even as our hearts pound and we worry about how we'll be received

Some relationships teach us how to be loved, how to let love in. How to allow ourselves to be supported. To ask for help and not see that as a weakness. To be looked after. To be cared for. To receive loving attention.

To be held in another's compassionate gaze. To let that compassion in. To know that we are so deserving of that.

Some connections teach us how to give support, to pay attention to another person's feelings and needs, to look after another. To take the lead and step in and step out of our own stuff. To give our time and attention, our emotional and physical strength. To offer the gift of our willing sacrifice. To discover our limits in the giving too. To give from a place of self-nourishment, not guilt.

Some relationships teach us the necessity of speaking up for ourselves. They force us to get honest about what's not okay for us, what hurts, what feels wrong, what feels like 'too much' or 'too little'. To become aware of when our boundaries have been crossed. To express our righteous anger, the part of us that feels unseen, unheard, not respected, abused. To respect ourselves enough to say "No", despite the consequences.

Sometimes we learn through break ups, heart-breaks, the death and transformation of relationships. We find the courage to take a step out of something that's unhealthy for us, step out of the old and into the unknown, step into aliveness, step into pain and feelings of loneliness maybe, step into our power and honour our precious hearts as they close and open and close and open and...

Sometimes we grow by staying in relationship

when we feel like leaving and stepping away. Staying present during conflict and misunderstanding, feeling our feelings of anger, fear, grief and exasperation, shame and guilt, expressing our painful or blissful truth. Finding power in the staying. Slowing down and looking together at the mess. Finding a place of reconnection, maybe. Making amends, maybe. Saying sorry, maybe. Owning our wounds and actions, and letting another own theirs.

Sometimes relationship teaches us how to be with another and sometimes it teaches us how to be with ourselves. How to stop running from our precious aloneness. To find the joy in silence, stillness, solitude.

To be One. To be two.

To unify. To separate.

To sense when we are out of balance.

To sense when we feel neglected.

Smothered.

Numb.

Disconnected.

Empty. Full

To take seriously our need to be alone.

To take seriously our need for companionship.

To know when we are hiding, afraid of being seen, avoiding connection.

To know when we are addictively abandoning ourselves for another, running from ourselves to meet another in co-dependency, expecting to be saved, fixed, mended, made whole.

Sometimes relationship is bliss.

Sometimes it is confusing, agonising.

We are called to touch the heights of intimacy.

We are called to touch the depths of our existential loneliness and deepest longings.

We are called to know ourselves.

All experiences on the path of relationship can teach us, change us, heal us.

Even in the struggle, we can find blessings and insights.

If we are willing to slow down and look.

If we are willing to stay curious and do the courageous work of softening into our embodied experience.

If we are willing to feel into the pains and pleasures of relating.

Deep in the tantric mud, we may strike gold.

28. THE DOORWAY OF THE SACRED ༄

What is trauma? Thoughts that feel unthinkable. Feelings that seem unbearable. Sensations in the body that we aren't able to fully hold and be with. Experiences we weren't able to fully digest when they originally happened. Pictures in the mind we just don't want to see. The darkness in ourselves that we run from, the 'negativity' that we hide from, conceal from ourselves and from others in fear and shame.

Moment by moment, we can begin to allow even the most terrifying and intense thoughts and feelings back into the healing arms of Now, where they belong.

In the presence of a loving friend, a skilled therapist, a great mountain, or the sky and all the gods and angels, with the ancient Earth holding us like a new-born, we can allow our defences to break, and touch into our deepest pain and sorrow, flushing it with curiosity, awareness, love.

Moment by moment in the great expanse of meditation we can begin to bear the unbearable, tolerate the intolerable, breathe through the deepest pain. Mindfully, slowly, we can flush the horror with light, drench the darkest regions with kindness, illuminate the Underworld, where the fearful and feral creatures dwell.

A wound is a portal. It will not kill you when you turn towards it. I have known horrors within myself that have pushed me to the edge of sanity, the edge of mortality. I have touched into grief so unbearable it felt like my heart couldn't hold one more second of it. I have felt rage so volcanic it could destroy or create an entire Cosmos.

But, moment by moment, I was able to bear the unbearable, accept the unacceptable, fall in love with the inner 'enemy'. An enemy that turned out to be an innocent inner child, screaming and raging for my love. My own flesh and blood. Not an enemy or alien, but *a part of myself*. This understanding changed my life forever.

At the core of my deepest trauma I saw my own kind face, smiling back at me. I found power and courage I never knew I had. I found the ultimate safety. I found God herself. She had used my deepest wounds (her own wounds) to call me back to myself (herself), and restore me to wholeness. No more separation.

Your trauma is a black hole. It will suck the life out of you and everyone around you if you try to run from it. But trauma can also be a quasar, an astonishing dynamo of new life, fuelled by the blackness, emitting more light than twenty galaxies.

Out of the darkness, light! Out of the pain, joy! Out of the alchemical fire, gold!

29. THE WILD BUDDHA 🪶

You can throw away the ideal of the "calm, cool, collected and rational one" right now, friend. You can let the image of the "perfectly peaceful stone Buddha" burn on the fire. It is a terrible lie. It is healthy to sob, to scream, to moan, to sigh, to laugh hysterically, to tremble, to feel fear, anger, profound sorrow, ecstatic joy, deep and powerful desires and longings.

There is a wild Buddha in all of us and she will not be tamed. The more you try to suppress her, the louder she gets. The more you try to shame her, try to make her feel crazy, 'irrational' or 'overly emotional', the angrier and more powerful she gets. The more you run from her, the more she runs after you. She will not be defeated with clever words and sophisticated philosophies. She will not be silenced; you will not be able to escape her, for you are only trying to escape yourself.

We all must eventually turn to face the Wild One inside, become curious about our natural feelings, urges and impulses, both pleasurable and painful, both gentle and intense, give them the gift of our mindful attention and breath, give them our love and understanding, give them a permanent home in ourselves, a place to roam freely. When we befriend our own wildness, we can befriend it in others. When we no longer fear our feelings, we will no longer—in vain—try to control the feelings of others, and we will have much compassion for our wild playmates. We will sob, scream, moan, sigh, laugh hysterically, tremble, feel fear, anger, profound sorrow, ecstatic joy, deep and powerful desires and longings together, and we will finally celebrate all of these as expressions of the Divine.

The Buddha sobbed like a baby sometimes, felt righteous anger at the injustice and abuse in the world, feared death but stood fearlessly at the heart of that fear. Here was the source of the Buddha's power—an infinite and unbreakable love for the wildness inside.

One of the greatest of all misunderstandings is that we "shouldn't be upset". Perhaps we learned from our parents, or from our spiritual gurus, therapists, self-help or religious teachers that we should always be *peaceful, calm and centred*—like them. We should be *relaxed, grounded, balanced, positive, happy*. And of course, we should always be *compassionate, kind, tolerant, selfless, accepting and deeply loving* towards each other. Anger was seen as a *negative* or *destructive* emotion, and we had to learn to go beyond it.

Beautiful ideals. Beautiful dreams. But here's the thing: Our inner child couldn't give a sh*t sometimes about being "good". Or "nice". Or "loving". Or "compassionate". Or even "happy".

And it has never even heard of "spirituality".

There is a beautifully narcissistic inner one who feels hurt, angry, scared, disgusted sometimes. Who feels unloved, unseen and neglected. And when we silence this inner one, repress and suffocate it, it boils with fiery rage from deep within the unconscious. It is innocent and only raging for loving attention—but we are not taught this. We are taught to fear our rage, hide it from ourselves, and from the world, in our quest to be *nice and good and happy… and very spiritual*.

It is this very *suppression* and *rejection* of our

deepest feelings that creates all suffering and violence in the world, not the feelings themselves, which are natural and harmless energies that just want to move in us to completion, and leave us in peace.

In its quest to be heard, in its attempt to attract our attention, the rage of the forgotten little one inside begins to drain us of our life energy, leaving us depressed, lethargic, exhausted, making us want to hide from life. The repressed rage feeds our addictions and compulsions. It generates stress, chronic pain and tension in the body, feeds disease and even generates suicidal and homicidal urges, which we in turn repress, deny or try to silence, all in our quest to maintain an acceptable picture of 'self'.

We cannot destroy or cut out this inner one. He is only crying out for the love he never received in childhood. The more we try to destroy him, the more he tries to destroy us. What we fear and fight in ourselves will only grow in power.

Great healing can happen when we let go of our mind-made ideals, and turn to face our living truth.

We admit that we are not full of "love and light and bliss" as we had pretended to be—but we are full of struggle today. This admission is like a death for the ego, a terrible defeat for the forces of fear and repression... but an absolute relief for our authentic selves.

We invite all the buried rage up into consciousness, so we can finally meet it. We connect with the furious inner one, hold him in our arms at last, let him exist, and live, and express in safe ways. Ask him what he needs, deep down. Does he feel unloved, disappointed, sad, forgotten? Does he feel neglected, abused, abandoned, unsafe? What vulnerability was the rage trying to bring our attention to? Let us shower this precious little one inside with fascinated attention, and give him a home and a voice. So he no longer controls us. So we can finally be his parent, not his slave.

When we befriend our anger, when we breathe into it, when we soothe it with a kind awareness, there can be great joy, the joy of true intimacy with ourselves. And we may discover a peace that is not the opposite of anger, but is right there at its core. The peace that comes from holding ourselves close, and celebrating all that we are, celebrating the great power of anger which rises intelligently to protect us from harm, perceived or actual.

Anger is not bad, wrong or a sign of our weakness or failure. It is a precious orphan child knocking on the door of the Present Moment, longing to be let in.

Your anger, doubts, sorrows and fears are not 'wrong' or 'bad' or 'unevolved'. They are not 'low vibrational' or 'negative' or 'unspiritual'. Those words are all labels and judgements of the mind. The Heart knows no such labels or judgements. Prior to all of these conceptual overlays, these feelings are only lost and lonely energies in us longing for warmth, acceptance, empathy, oxygen, and curious attention.

Fear is *not* the opposite of love, just as no wave is the 'opposite' of the ocean. Fear is a complete expression of consciousness, the same ocean-consciousness that dances as bliss and joy and wonder too. Fear is a contracted, tense, dense and held-in form of love, but not its 'opposite'.

This non-dual understanding will change your life. And begin to end all inner opposition and violence.

You do not 'attract' abuse, loss or misfortune through a faulty 'vibrational frequency'. You did not manifest your cancer or infection or fracture through your desires. These are old guilt-ridden, victim-shaming—and frankly narcissistic—stories based on a dualistic understanding.

We need these New Age myths and lies no longer. Let us turn to face reality instead, and welcome all feelings, even the 'darkest' ones, as our beloved inner

children, waves of the Heart, astonishing expressions
of the Divine.

Sometimes I look around this world and a great and ancient sadness moves through me. Everything and everyone moves so damn *fast* here. I feel like an alien, often. A slow, mindful, present alien. I watch people rushing from experience to experience, barely stopping to contemplate the miracle of their existence, hardly ever taking time to let the wonder in. Going for days and days without ever feeling their feelings. Running from themselves addictively, towards imaginary futures. So mesmerised by the *there* that they forget the miracle of *here*. So identified with the *doing* that the most precious thing is lost. *The simple feeling of being alive.*

Comfortable. Popular. Fabulous and successful, perhaps. On the path towards a better and exciting tomorrow, perhaps. Yet so afraid to slow down, to rest deeply, to stop and invite in whatever lurks in the depths of the unconscious. The repressed terrors. The anxieties. Unmetabolised childhood yearnings. Unlived lives, unfulfilled potentials, unspoken truths. In love with the light yet afraid to touch the darkness. Forgetting the natural joy of being, the inner child that was squashed so we could become 'grown ups'. Neglecting the playfulness which had to be numbed in order to 'fit in'. And now, content with surface pleasures. Success. Popularity. Looks. Achievements. The things that matter but don't truly matter in the end. Satisfied with a limited, conditional version of happiness. The kind you can post on Instagram. The kind that you can buy and sell. The kind that has an opposite and can crumble so quickly. The kind that looks good.

It's sad to see our great potential forgotten. Nothing 'wrong' with any of this unconscious activity, of course. I certainly do not sit in judgement over my fellow humans. I have been completely unconscious in my time. I love our vulnerable humanity, and understand the mechanism of running, and we are all only doing our best, given our conditioning and our inherited and conditioned fear of ourselves. I used to run. But I had to break down. For the love I sought could never be found in the future. It was always here, buried in my own Heart, much closer than breathing.

I only wish that everyone could truly find the courage to stop. Rest. Break, if they need to. Cry, if they need to. And finally *feel*: the abandonment, the grief, the shame that was unconsciously running the show. Finally stop pretending. Finally sacrifice the addictive surfaces for the living truth—the scary, disorienting, thrilling, embarrassing, awkward, groundless truth.

There is no shame in breaking and in breathing through the mess.

To be slow and empathic in a fast world, it is a challenge for sure. To be sensitive in a world that has gone mad with goals and results, insane with surfaces and statistics. To be a lover in a world that has reduced love to a commodity. To be awake in a world that tries to numb you and then tries to sell you medications and cures and distractions for your numbness.

Yet *you* cannot be numbed. You know your path now, and you cannot turn back. And your sensitivity is a great gift to this fast world. You can teach the world how to slow down, how to behold the beauty in the ordinary and the mundane, how to be comfortable with space and silence and not knowing, how to breathe…

33. WALKING WITH JOY

Sometimes you become so mesmerised by the goal, the destination, the future, the 'place you should be', that you forget the present ground, the place where you stand, the place from which you will take the next step, the place where life always is.

You forget that you are breathing now, that the journey is made only of breaths, fleeting instants, moments that cannot be repeated. You forget your own presence, so solid, so trustworthy, so constant amidst the constant change of the journey. The destination has become more important than presence, and you have become lost in time.

Joy is not a place you reach. Joy will not appear magically on the completion of your journey. Joy lives only in presence. Joy has a home called Now.

Joy is there in the sense of being alive, the belly rising and falling, the pounding of the heart, the surprising sounds of the afternoon. Joy is there in every step taken or not taken. Whether you are lost, or far from your destination, or unsure about your next step, joy is there, walking with you, breathing down your neck, willing you on.

34. LOVE'S ADVENTURE 🖋

We long for love as much as we fear it. We yearn to be seen as much as we bolt at the possibility of being seen. We hunger for the deep embrace of intimacy, tender eyes that gaze upon us with understanding and empathy, as much as we try to avoid that very gaze. It's too risky. Too exposing. Nowhere to hide. *To be seen is to die.*

A battle rages in us. The unloved one longing to hide, and the one who longs for the thrill and risk and adventure of loving.

Unconsciously, we are attracted to or repelled by those who treat us, speak to us, hold us the way our parents did or did not. We are drawn to those who can heal us, and sometimes drawn to those who cannot. We think we are falling in love with a person, and sometimes we are just falling in love with our own image of them, which has nothing to do with them at all.

We love and we lose our images of love. We rise and we fall. Our hearts soar and our hearts break into a million pieces. We seek security and find insecurity and we find security in that. We seek freedom and find the prison of our own programming and lose hope and then regain it.

Sometimes it takes courage to leave a relationship. Sometimes it takes courage to stay. Sometimes it takes courage to do nothing, today. Sometimes it takes courage to admit how much pain you are in. Sometimes it takes courage to admit how happy you are.

Sometimes you take a step without knowing why, and everything only becomes clear in hindsight. You can't get it wrong anyway. *Take the step, or do not,* love whispers.

We lose ourselves and we find ourselves. We give more than we can take, exhausting ourselves in the name of "love". Or we run as fast as we can, exhausting ourselves in our flight from "love".

"Will somebody see me. Listen. Hold me. Let me break..."

And the drama of love plays out. And as the play goes on we learn more about ourselves. We begin to see our blind spots. Our unconscious patterns come into the light of awareness. We realise our assumptions. Our childhood fantasies start to crumble. Pain that we never wanted to feel, we suddenly feel. Grief. Anger. Feelings of rejection, abandonment, shame. We want to run, go back into the old addictions, the old comfort, and for whatever reason, we don't. We get curious. We start looking and stop thinking so much. We begin to relate to ourselves. Treat ourselves like the greatest lovers that we are. The most fascinating and beloved creatures.

With each day, we begin meeting ourselves more deeply. Discovering who we really are. What we feel, and what we don't. What we want and what we don't. Learning to say 'yes' when we mean yes and 'no' when we mean no and if that hurts someone, giving them back their responsibility to heal. Learning that love is not all butterflies and roses and positive feelings. It is work, too. It is mess. It is pain and the courage to breathe through that pain into joy and expansiveness. Love asks us to become more and more real, more and more human, more and more conscious, less and less perfect. More self-aware and willing to feel. And to feel more. And to feel more. And more. And to let our hearts break sometimes. To not know, sometimes. To be bored, sometimes. To be blissed-out, sometimes. To be full of life, sometimes. To sometimes not know what the next step is. And to then take it, or not.

Love is not a feeling, a state, or an experience. It's not a destination. It's this extraordinary Light that shines from within. It's this radiant Knowing that never leaves. It's the Joy of being alive.

We can know it together. We can know it alone. We can remind each other of it. We can forget, too. We can trigger each other and help each other to become curious about those triggers. We can do that work, or not.

We can meet in love's fire. Walk together, or not. Share our hearts. Step back. Step towards. Or stay where we are. Learn to love the dance of it, the spontaneity, the adventure, the mystery, the immediacy and the intimacy of it and the running too. Learn to unlearn what we know and embrace the unknowing as new knowing. And get more and more content with the unresolvability of it all. More and more happy with the unhappy one, certain about the uncertainty, so secure in the insecurity. More and more blissed-out at our lack of bliss. More and more curious about what's here Now. Less and less solid, more and more playful. Less a seeker of love, more a giver of it, and a finder of it, and a wild Presence that invites others into the same joy.

This is Love's Adventure, in each and every moment of our lives.

35. THE SWEETNESS OF THE HEART'S REOPENING 🖎

Sweetheart, I know your heart feels closed right now.

You feel lonely, disconnected, separate, like you're not part of this world, and the things that brought you joy yesterday seem so far away today. I want you to know you are still precious, still an astonishing movement of creation, still fascinating and beautiful as you are, even with your closed and aching heart.

Bring your attention to the here-and-now; past and future are not your true home, my love. Become curious about your body. Feel its weight, its warmth. Do some parts of your body feel tight, pressured, heavy? Is there a deadness, a constricted feeling somewhere? Do some regions feel expansive, spacious, light, tingly? Is there a hollow feeling in the belly? A tightness in the throat? A constricted feeling between the eyes? Is the jaw tense or relaxed? What is the quality of your breathing in this moment? What sounds do you hear around you now? What is the loudest sound you can hear? What is the closest sound, and the furthest sound? Can you become curious about this moment, this present scene in the movie of your life, see it the way a child would? Can you witness it, without judging it or trying to change it? Can this moment be the way it is, and if it can't, can that be allowed, too? Can even your resistance to this moment be allowed, your non-acceptance, your "no", your refusal of what is? Can *everything* be given a place, here? The sorrow, the loneliness, the exhaustion, the heaviness and frustration, even the despair? Can it all be held in the moment, the way a mother holds her precious new-born?

Can it be okay
for you to
not be okay, now?

Perhaps there is no mistake, my dear. Perhaps nothing is going wrong. Perhaps the story the mind has constructed about life is just that, a story, and you are here, whole, prior to all stories. Perhaps you are not supposed to know, ever, and perhaps the heart *has* to close sometimes, to protect itself, to rest and to rejuvenate, and for you to eventually know the sweetness of its reopening.

Perhaps you are more *alive* than you ever thought possible.

The truth will always come out.

You can try to suppress truth, you can threaten, punish, enslave, crucify those who dare speak it, you can run from it, try to numb it, silence it, smother it, shame it, ridicule it, throw all manner of lies and manipulations and half-truths at it.

But in the end, truth will always win. Because truth is life.

And it takes courage to speak truth. You may risk losing your livelihood, your relationships, your reputation, your worldly possessions, your friends, your family, even your life. You may be quaking as you speak it, dripping with sweat, nauseous and dry-mouthed and on the verge of fleeing.

But in the end you cannot hold it back. It is more powerful than you. It will outlast you and outlive you. You were born from it and will return to it. It speaks through you; you are a vessel for truth. And when you know truth and declare it to the Universe and to all who will listen, you may feel the doubt and the guilt and the shame of it too, the terror of abandonment, old thoughts warning you to shut the hell up.

But you will feel so alive. So on your path. So aligned with your calling. So willing to face the consequences, moment by moment, breath by breath. And those who want your truth will gather around you, and you will know your true family.

There is no greater power on Earth, no more potent agent for change, and no more thrilling experience, than you, wild and alive with your truth.

Let's not commit right now to a future together, my love. The future is so unknown, and we are so fluid and alive and ever-changing, and tired of pretending that we know.

Let's commit to *Presence*. Let's commit to *meeting*, in the fire of today. To *knowing* each other and letting ourselves be known. To *walking* this path of healing, wherever it may take us.

To *telling the truth to ourselves and to each other.*

Our thoughts and feelings are ever-changing within us, and uncontrollable, like a wild ocean of love. Our desires wax and wane; our dreams are born and die in every moment. Let's not commit to a form of love, today. The forms are always shifting, like the tides. We do not need the old security now. Let's make a deeper commitment; one that cannot be broken or lost. *To love itself.* To presence. To meeting in the here-and-now. To bringing and showing all of ourselves. To telling the truth, today; knowing that our truth may change tomorrow. To listening to each other. To bowing before each other's experience, even if our hearts are broken and tender, even if we trigger the deepest pain in each other, the most profound disappointment, the strongest urges and longings.

Let us commit to meeting our own pain. Loving

each other takes courage! Yes! For love is a field, not a form. Let us commit to the field, remember the field in every moment of our precious days on this Earth, devote ourselves to the field, the eternal Now.

In ten years' time, we may still be together. We may have children. We may live together, or live apart. We may never see each other again. This may be our last day. If we are honest, *we really do not know*; not knowing is our Home. When our eyes are open, when we are awake, we live very close to life, very close to death, very close to insecurity, very close to loss. But this is where we find such great aliveness—on the edge of things. Where everything is always new. Where we are constantly surprised by ourselves, and each other.

We may be friends, or lovers, or strangers, or family, or we may remain undefined, beyond narrative, our love unable to be captured in words. Here at the edge of the known, on the line that once divided sanity from madness, and doubt from certainty, we play, we dance, we drink tea, we touch each other, we cry, we laugh, we meet. We sacrifice comfort and predictability. But what we gain is astonishing: *This tremendous sense of being alive.* No longer numb to the mysteries of love, the mysteries of our bodies. A little raw, perhaps. A little shaky. Maybe a little disoriented, but perhaps this is the price of being totally free. Maybe an old part of us still seeks mommy or daddy, that Magic Person who will never leave, give us all the answers and take away the terrible loneliness repressed in our guts. Loving that frightened part too; bowing to that part too, but no longer being controlled by it.

And they will ask: *What about your future? Why are you afraid of commitment? Why do you run from security? Comfort? Future? Convention? The Known?* They will say you are crazy, or you don't understand love, or you are lost, or you are unloving and selfish, and you will smile, and understand their fear, for their fear was once yours, and you cannot abandon your path now. And nobody has to walk with you. Ever.

At some point, only Truth will satisfy. A living Truth, renewing itself each and every moment, the wild Truth of the heart.

When Love and Truth are One, when the Commitment is deeply rooted in the breath, we can finally face each other without resentment, and explode into the most melancholy sunsets, held in the most profound joy.

Walking alone, together, alone.

38. LONELINESS CONTAINS ITS OWN CURE

The more you surrender into presence, that existential freedom which is your birthright and your true home, and the more you relax out of the mind and its infinitely complex conditioning, and the more you shed those roles and activities you habitually use to escape yourself, the more you will encounter the raw longings, anxieties and insecurities you were always running from.

You were always seeking security in an inherently insecure cosmos.

The less identified with the narrative you become, the more groundless and homeless you may begin to feel. But this is not a bad thing. Groundlessness is the way, the truth, the life; it is how pure freedom can be intimately known. As the Buddha taught, there is no ground anywhere to be found. Nothing to hold onto. No home. No rest for the seeker. *Except* here in presence. *Except* in the breath. *Except* in this field of true acceptance. The mind is no ground for you.

There is a profound loneliness and sense of loss inherent in the experience of freedom. It is the loneliness of pure meditation, the loss of a solid world; it is the loneliness of distant planets spinning in infinite night. It is the loneliness of forever being at the point of pure creation. It is the loneliness of leaving the known world and confronting the precious passing moments. It is the loneliness that exists at the core of every being, the loneliness that is the realisation, "I am living and I am dying and I cannot resolve this Mystery for myself, and nobody can resolve it for me, and nobody can breathe for me, love for me, die for me..."

This is a sacred loneliness, a holy sense of loss that is not bad, or wrong, or dangerous, or sinful or shameful, or a sign that you are broken or damaged or incomplete in some way; it is actually a nourishing, comforting, restful, life-giving energy, a misunderstood doorway to peace, to self-love, to contentment and joy. It is a loneliness that never leaves, that is not dependent on how many people surround you or how 'popular' you are or how many 'fans' you have, a loneliness that is actually built-in to Being itself, that calls you home moment by moment. Back here. To the body. To the earth. To the day as it unfolds. To the wonder of things. To the achingly green *green* of the grass in springtime. To the impossibly blue *blue* of the summer sky. To the mind-stopping awe of creation. To the beauty you cannot begin to put into words, the beauty that only exists for a moment, the beauty that you cannot grasp.

Out of the mind and into this presence! To this intimacy with life. This is a loneliness that does not separate you or isolate you, but actually connects you profoundly with all things. It is a healthy loneliness, and it takes courage and strength to stay near to it and not run away into habitual distractions.

It is the kind of loneliness that everyone on the path of true meditation must confront in the end.

And so when you stop fleeing to your addictions designed to help you 'escape' from loneliness, and instead become intimate with this loneliness, nurture it, hold it close, breathe lovingly into it, understand it, converse with it, invite it in, paint it and sing it and dance it, you then understand the loneliness of every human heart, the unresolvable longing for God and rest and love and safety at the core of everyone's being, and your heart cracks open with compassion, *and you are not lonely anymore.* You come out of the story of separation, the great movie called "I Have Been Abandoned", and you connect very deeply with the exquisite soft and friendly loneliness of being that is pure freedom.

You meet "the lonely one" inside and you love it so it is no longer lonely.

You touch life at the point of creation.

Loneliness contains its own cure. Dive in.

I should have liked to have met you, Vincent. To have stood there with you on that threshold where formless becomes form, to have held you there on that dizzying precipice where we enter life and are entered in return, no protection, no answers. The field all true artists know, fear, are attracted to, flee then return to in the end because they have no other choice but to *participate*. The field where self and world and other dissolve and there are only sunflowers of brilliant yellow and eternities of dancing wheat and shimmering skies bursting with stars and roaring seas crazy with blue and white and every shade of green and nowhere to call home except there in the seeing itself. A world on the edge of tears, on the edge of stars, nobody to understand except the one who stops trying.

The seeing. The seeing! A hair's breadth from madness, a hair's breadth from ecstasy! I should have liked to have held you there, my friend. Reminded you that you were safe. That your loneliness was sacred and your despair was not shameful and even your darkest secrets, urges and fantasies were not mistakes, not damn mistakes or signs of your failure or evidence of your sickness or proof that you weren't meant for this world. No, your human flaws were nothing less than art, *the art of the future* as you called it, where the peasant is king and the most ordinary moment has vastness in it. The future art of seeing every damn shade of our imperfect humanity as an expression of divinity, the same divinity that animated those wheat fields you disappeared into for days on end, painting, always painting, forever painting. Your *feelings* were sunflowers too, you see, your joy and your pain were as great and alive as those starry skies and seas all bursting with colour and light and shocking movement, and all the strange sensations surging through your body, all the traumas you were never quite able to touch, they were beautiful, too, Vincent, and safe. To me, anyway. And to many others who walk this strange path of awakening. You had a family you never met. I wish we had met.

In a wheat field in Auvers one cool summer evening you lost all hope or perhaps you intuited a hope so vast and unreachable that it finally broke your spirit and you shot yourself through the chest with a revolver and two days later in a little attic room, your heart stopped and you became infinite. Or the infinite took you back, back to your beloved wheat fields but now inseparable from them, back to light, back to mother, back Home, and you found the deepest kind of rest you had never fully known in your short life.

In that tiny room they surrounded you with sunflowers and yellow dahlias and your last paintings, and they wept and remembered, and no church could have contained you anyway.

You were 37 then.

Oh, I don't think you were mad. I think you were too alive for this world. You were moved to tears by haystacks and potato eaters, prostitutes and tree roots. I think you saw too deeply and felt too keenly and found no home here because you were constantly torn asunder by the twin pulls of heaven and earth. And I think nobody had ever taught you how to hold yourself in-between the way you held the ever-shifting sunlight over those haystacks.

Oh. I just would have liked to have known you, my friend. That's all.

Thank you for your courage. Thank you for helping us see.

Thank you for the sunflowers, the irises, the wheat fields, the almond tree, the starry nights.

40. THE STILLNESS IN THE CHAOS

Your legs ache. You've been on your feet all day. You're in a long line waiting for the ticket machine. They've just announced your train is delayed. You feel the frustration mounting. Impatience, annoyance, despair.

Resistance to the moment, to the way things are.

Suddenly, you remember, you are breathing. And it is Now. And you only ever have to face a single Now. And you feel your tired feet rather than thinking about them. You give them a little attention, which is love. And you feel the frustration in your chest and belly rather than trying to delete these innocent sensations.

And you feel the weight of your body, the way it gently rests in gravity, supported by the sacred earth.

And you feel your belly expand, slowly, rising on the in-breath. Falling on the exhale. And all the sounds around you are now innocent; you are a soft microphone. And the thoughts whirring around in your head, they are just little birds, singing their songs, flapping away.

And it's all okay. It's all okay. It's all present. It's all okay.

Even though it's not okay, it's *okay*.

It's okay that life is like *this*, right now.

And you find gratitude again. You are alive, you have been given a day. A day to live. A day to breathe, and taste human experience, taste the joy and sorrow of it, taste train stations and ticket machines and the bliss and the boredom of it all, the frustration and the rush and the whirr of it, the silliness and the crash and the pull and the chaos of it.

You are already surrendered. And you find yourself on the train home, trusting some unfathomably ancient schedule.

41. THE PATH OF THE BROKEN HEART

"Clear up your vibration and you'll stop attracting bad things to yourself".

"If you have fears, if you are in resistance, if you have anger, doubts and shame, then you must be in your ego, and totally unenlightened".

"If you think there's a problem with someone's words or actions, you are always the one who's confused".

"Everything is just your projection. Everything is in your mind. Everything is unreal".

"You attracted your pain because you desired and deserved it".

"You are too attached to the body. Go beyond the body. It's not who you are."

"The past is an illusion. Let it go immediately!".

No, it's not *always* your projection. Sometimes you are seeing very clearly indeed.

No, everything isn't always "only in your mind". Sometimes you need to trust your gut instinct more, not less.

No, your doubts and fears are not a sign of your lack of spiritual evolution.

No, you do not attract abuse through a faulty 'vibrational frequency'.

No, you do not deserve to be violated in any way, in the name of truth, in the name of God, in the name of love, or in any other name. Your boundaries deserve to be respected, your 'yes' *and* your 'no' equally.

No, it's not okay for spiritual teachers to shame people "for their own good" (to shock them into awakening, to enlighten them, to help them drop their "ego").

I cannot support any spirituality that dismisses our tender, vulnerable, fragile humanity, that shames us for our precious human thoughts and feelings, that divides self from no self, sacred from human, holy from profane, absolute from relative, heaven from earth, duality from nonduality.

I once saw a popular spiritual teacher addressing a recently bereaved woman. He said, "Your heartbreak is totally unreal and only the activity of the separate self. You are pure Awareness, and nothing more. Your son, and his death, are just a convincing illusion of mind. One day the separate self will vanish, along with all suffering."

And in that moment, I saw a deep sickness and inhumanity at the heart of contemporary spirituality. The invalidation of trauma, the false promises, the power games, the suppression of the divine feminine.

And I vowed to bow to that broken heart as if it were God Herself.

Until the end of time.

42. A WILD DEVOTION TO A BURNING WORLD

We are the vessels, my love, the containers, the formless and the form. Galaxies birth themselves in our giant bellies! We are filled with the roar of lions, unfulfilled ancestral longings, mothers, sons, the living, the dead, the cries of a world yet unborn.

Our bodies intertwined now, sticky, sweaty, merging with the earth, penetrated by the earth, carbon, hydrogen, oxygen, the present moment collapsing into itself, space becoming infinite time, strange beasts fighting bloody limbs flying tearing shredding spraying spewing rupturing, nature devouring itself, death as life.

I am you and you are I, eternal.

We are the ones with hearts of thunder still, limbs of lightning. We will not settle for easy answers. We will stay close to the throb and pulse of life, the pounding and the shaking of it, the thunder and the light. We will break ourselves daily on the altar of experience, broken to pieces for love, broken and penetrated and broken over and over again relentlessly, ceaselessly, caught up in this erotic union until exhaustion, until the climax of more opening, always opening, non-stop entering and being entered, flooding and being flooded, with such power, with such pleasure, pain, bliss, melancholy, in an ecstatic dance of nearness and separation, love and longing, shadow and sun.

Prior to our clever philosophies, prior to the machines, prior to the Earth itself, let us meet here, in utter bewilderment that we exist, that we exist at all.

Yes, my love, they can shame us, call us uncivilised, lock us up, but they cannot take away our wildness, cannot break our devotion to a burning world!

43. HOW TO MEET FEAR

I was speaking with a young man who was plagued by
fear. He felt stuck in his life, creatively blocked, held
back by inner demons. He dreamed of writing a book,
sharing his truth and his art with the world. But every
time he contemplated taking the next step on the
sacred path of his heart, his whole body would seize
up, and his mind would go crazy with fear and shame.
So many images and voices in his head, warning him
to give up, imagining what would go wrong, and how
people would respond negatively to his art. He would
be rejected, judged and ridiculed, and that would be
too much to bear. It became overwhelming for him
to even think about doing what he loved. So he hid
from life and his calling, unable to leave his house
sometimes, paralysed and sad.

I asked him if he would be willing to take a step
with me into his deepest fear.

He said yes, he was willing.

I invited him to bring awareness to all the voices
and images in his head, to be the space in which all
this mind-activity could arise. He didn't need to get
rid of the voices, or silence them, just see them as old
voices from childhood, shaming and fearful voices that
were actually only trying to "protect" him, keep him
small and safe. (Ultimately they were not even 'his'
thoughts and voices, they were voices his father and

mother heard, and their parents, and their parents. Ancestral voices, not even his own). As an adult, Now, in the safety of Presence, with me, he could hear these voices, see these scary images, and not take them as the Truth, just creative displays of mind.

He could say, "Thank you, mind, for your suggestions, your imagined futures, your fears. But I will not be your slave any longer."

I asked him to turn his attention now to his body. What sensations wanted to be met? Where did this 'fear' live? He spoke of a profound heaviness in his belly and chest, a sense of contraction and pressure that had been with him for as long as he could remember. I invited him to be fully present with those sensations that he named 'fear', without trying to fix or heal them, or make them go away. I invited him to give them space, allow them to live; to breathe into them, flush them through with oxygen, bless them with loving attention.

He told me that, as he gave loving attention to them, the sensations began to intensify and move. The energy was going upwards in his body.

"The energy is coming into my throat, into my head..."

"Good, just allow that. Allow the energy to move. It's safe..."

"It's all over me now... Ugh.... It's throughout my whole body, the fear, it's like a virus spreading..."

"Okay, yes! Yes. Stay with it. Breathe into it all. It just wants to move, to be met. Trust this..."

"No! I can't take it anymore! This fear.... it's going to kill me. It's going to..."

"John, are you still alive, now? Right now?

I could see him come out of his mind, out of his scary thought-constructed future, and back into the safety of his body, the safety of the Now that we shared together.

"Yes. I'm here."

"Then it hasn't killed you yet. Are you alive Now?"

"Yes."

"Yes... Now... Now... Now... You're still here with me... You're still alive..."

I could see him starting to think about his fear again...

"I hate it. I HATE IT! I'M GOING TO......"

"Yes! And you're still here, Now. I'm here with you John. We are here. Just allow..."

And suddenly, all his resistance to the fear fell away. He stopped thinking about the future and dropped deeply into his body, and into Trust. The fear was still present and alive in him, but now he was bigger than it. He was not in the fear, it was in him. He was holding the fear—it was not holding him any longer.

He was the space for fear.

"See, you're allowing all this fear, and you're still alive, and breathing! This is your power, your ability to be present with fear, to hold it, make room for it..."

"I'm still here. It didn't kill me. I thought I was going to die."

"How do you feel now, John??"

"Shaky... warm... tingly... alive..."

He had found the courage to face the Unbearable within him. And he had been able to bear it, beautifully, effortlessly.

"Yes. Now you know. You know how to meet fear. Stare it in the face. Be present with it. Trust it. Let it move in you to completion. Fear is *safe*. Your body knows what to do. Fear can't hurt you, John. It can be intense, uncomfortable, scary, of course, but it can't hurt Who You Truly Are."

"Yes. Yes. I can feel my whole body now, it's warm and shaky and vibrating with life. I've never felt this way before..."

I received an email from John a month or so later. He had started work on his book. He had even started a blog, begun to share some of his words with others. Yes, sometimes the old fears would come up—voices in the head and uncomfortable sensations in the body —but now he was willing and able to be *present* with these frightened parts of himself as they arose. And he was able to *keep writing* through the fear. The fear did not have to block him or hold him back from his calling. Fear could be an ally on his hero's journey, not his enemy any longer, but something he could meet and be curious about and drench with playful awareness when it came to visit. The fearful little boy inside him was not a mistake, a disease, or a problem to be fixed, but something to be loved, embraced, blessed, even celebrated, when he came to visit.

John had turned to meet his deepest fear, confronted the Dark Thing he imagined would destroy him... and instead, it had brought new life, new creativity.

44. THE BELOVED

I must confess something. I am a murderer.

Wait, hold on. Do not be shocked. I am only telling you something you already knew way before your parents were born.

I am a murderer. I am a saint. I am a prostitute. I am a thief. I am the homeless man rummaging through the trash cans by the gas station you pass every night on the way home from work. I am a vandal. I am an artist. I am a wild lover. I am all the oceans. I am creation and destruction. I am the galaxies and the stars.

I am a giraffe. I am Mickey Mouse. I am the starving child on the TV with those hollow, staring eyes you cannot look into for long before your heart starts breaking. I am everything that moves you and everything that leaves you stone cold. I am American Idol. I am Mozart's Magic Flute. I am as vast as a Universe. I am tinier than the tiniest sub-sub-atomic particle. I am silent, yet I am as loud as seven thousand apocalypses.

I take all forms, yet I cling to no particular form.

I do not say "I am form". I do not say "I am not form".

I do not say "I exist". I do not say "I do not exist".

I do not call myself God, consciousness, awareness, presence, spirit... or even Life.

I have no name for myself. I am anonymous.

Yet all names are my own.

Humans fight and kill and die over the names they gave me.

They form religions, dogmas, systems of thought. They claim I am on their "side" (I take no sides). They say I belong to them (I belong to nobody and everybody). They try to figure me out. They even claim to be me, know me, channel me. Some of them claim to have found The One Path that leads to me. They always have, they always will.

They do not know. Their minds are way too limited.

Yet 'mind' is one of my many ingenious appearances.

I appear as everything, yet when you stop and look for me, you cannot find me. I play in the cosmic hide and seek. I sometimes appear when you stop looking altogether.

I am these words, and all the spaces between them. I am the silence at the end of the sentences... and the expectation at their beginning. I am the black and the white of it, and every shade of grey, and every colour too. I am the understanding and the lack of understanding. I am the similarity and the contrast. I am the separation and the unspeakable unity.

I am the eyes moving across this page and the page moving across these eyes. I am the seeing and all that is seen. I do not divide myself between subject and object. Separation is not my religion. I know nothing of 'I', yet I speak of 'I' for the simple joy of it.

I am male and I am female. I am East and West. I am inside and outside. I speak every language fluently. I am all that is, all that has been, and all that will ever be. I am now, and never now. I cannot be reduced to anything. Eternities pass in the space of a breath. Aeons are my lifeblood.

I am breathing you now.

I am the in-breath and the out-breath of you. I am every sacred, intimate breath.

I am every one of your thoughts arising and dissolving in the vastness.

I am every feeling surging like a comet through the universal body.

I am sorrow. I am anger. I am fire. I am water.

I am always here, whether I am recognised or not.

I am the "Am" even when the I is not.

I am nothing and everything, nobody and everybody.

I am the murderer. The murderer says "I am".

I am the saint. The saint says "I am".

I am the prostitute. The prostitute says "I am".

I am the child. The child says "I am".

I am the scientist. The scientist says "I am".

I am the dying man. The dying man says "I am".

The story of "I" is always different, yes. That is my creativity.

But "Am" is always the same. AM. OM. That is my unchanging nature.

Do not seek me. Do not look for me in time. Do not be proud that you have found me. I am not your trophy. I am not food for your hungry spiritual ego. Simply admit that I am already here. Admit that I have always been here. And live your life as a constant remembrance of me. Devote yourself to the joy of being me. Let your life be your love song to me. Let your actions and words express me, bring me into form.

I am your deepest wisdom. I am closer than your most profound aloneness.

I have never abandoned you, I will never abandon you, I do not know abandonment.

I will be here when you take your final breath.

You are my beloved child.

I was there at your birth, holding you.

Do you remember?

45. I SHALL GIVE YOU MORE OF MY MAD SELF 🖋️

Words are like ice cream.

I mean, the kind of ice cream they give to astronauts.

Dad bought me some in the gift shop of the Science Museum when I was seven. It came in a shiny grey foil packet. It was dry and smelled like sour milk and the future. I think it was his way of apologising for everything else.

I have poetry in my head all day, you know. 99.9% of it never gets out. Giving it form would suck the life from it. At least that's what I tell myself.

Thirty years later I knelt by dad's bed and sang to him. I imagined that he heard me. Maybe he was too far gone. Way out in space.

I enjoyed singing anyway.

The nurse came in and told me to "stay strong". I didn't know what she meant. I was drenched with tears and happy beyond reason because nothing was wrong anymore. My tears were my strength.

When you're a hundred thousand miles from Earth, maybe ice cream that crumbles is better than no ice cream at all.

All right then. You win. I shall give you more of my mad self.

46. EXODUS

Would you look? And if you looked, would you even see?

An old man and a boy, the sea, a weathered café, all doilies and yellowing flyers for tribute acts on the promenade, the music faded now but still the lingering promise of something good. Toasted cheese sandwiches, coffee rings on Formica, bits of crisps under table legs, all the faces that silently watch for hours.

A crumb hangs on the old man's lower lip, a speck of saliva on his chin. Waiting to fall, both.

The old man is watching the boy, squinting as if he sees something buried deep in him. The boy is gazing out of the window, watching a bird peck at a blue carrier bag in the sand, its handles tied in a knot. I think a record by Cliff Richard is playing. I can't be sure. It is all soft treble and tin now, disappearing into the static and bass of the ocean. Maybe it's *Congratulations*.

I think I am the boy, and I think you are the old man. I think we had that last day together.

The sun shifts out of view behind clouds heavy with evening. A shadow swoops along the promenade like the Angel of Death in that bible movie we watched together when I was young enough to believe that we could part great waters and the first born would be saved, and you kept getting up to make me sweet milky tea. These things I won't forget although you have forgotten. I get a shiver that's somewhere between cold, dehydration and low blood sugar. It's been a long day shifting from café to café, listening to you yawn and complain about cafés and dry cakes and the length of days.

"Why don't you put your jacket on, dad. It's getting chilly."

"I didn't bring my jacket."

"It's on your chair. Behind you."

He twists in his seat, touches the scrunched hood hanging over the chair's back.

"Not mine, son."

Wait.

"Ah. So it is."

It always is.

He folds himself into the jacket. God, he's so small now. Dad, shrinking. You never expect dads to shrink, just jackets.

Time passes. Yawning. I don't know if it's silence or just the absence of words. Or perhaps we are waiting for something yet to be named.

Two seagulls attack a tuna baguette in the sand.

Suddenly, without warning. "You know, son, you're a good boy."

He reaches over. He never reaches over. I'm a good boy, he says. He touches my left hand. It feels hard, dry, like something eroded over billions of years, closer now to its essence. So many liver spots, unexplored crevices, ridges as deep as all that is unspoken in him, things in his heart he could never share.

"We are on different paths, son. That's okay. You're a good boy."

He squeezes. For a moment I can hardly breathe.

We are on different paths, and it's okay, and I'm a good boy.

Seagulls fighting over the tuna baguette, its contents exploding now, tearing into lettuce, mashed tuna, flashes of white, yellow, red, frenzied bird eyes.

"Yes, dad. It's okay."

"What's that, son?"

"I said, it's okay that we're on different paths."

"Huh? Oh. Yes, yes."

He looks away. The seagulls give up, flap to the place along the promenade where the light moved.

He wipes his mouth with the side of his hand and gravity takes the crumbs.

He yawns.

"Funny-looking birds, aren't they?"

"Yeah, dad. They're funny, those birds."

'Congratulations, and celebrations, when I tell everyone that you're in love with me. Congratulations, and jubilations, I want the world to know I'm happy as can be.' The kind of song they play in places like this, this time of year, on days like this one.

We are like kings, I think.

There is no language of the holy
The sacred lies in the ordinary

—Deng Ming-Dao

✿ about New Sarum Press

Established in 2019, New Sarum Press is Julian and Catherine Noyce's second publishing venture. Their first, Non-Duality Press, was acquired in 2015 by New Harbinger Publications, San Francisco, USA, where it continues to flourish as a discrete imprint.

With the same degree of integrity, at New Sarum Press we are committed to offering books which address the ongoing dialogue between the traditions of Eastern wisdom and Western philosophy and psychology. Non-Duality Press was one of the earliest publishers to unpack and explore the contemporary expression of awakening and enlightenment. It also asked if these concepts are definable, valuable or even ultimately misleading.

New Sarum Press has a wider remit. We still publish the leading guides of the consciousness movement but we are open to books on the perennial philosophy, the counter-culture and its history and the healing arts and therapies. The question we ask of any submitted manuscript is, 'is this book accessible and relevant to our readers?' And, 'is this an original and positive contribution to personal growth and wellbeing as well as the wider healing of the planet?'

Unlike some larger publishers, we work as partners with our authors, we divide the income from book sales equally and offer them our many years of experience in the niche publishing industry.

Titles currently in print

REAL-WORLD NONDUALITY
Reports From The Field

Eleven new writers tell us how the 'direct path' approach as described by Sri Atmananda Krishna Menon (1883 –1959) became woven into their daily lives. None of the writers are claiming enlightenment or liberation and yet we can each find something in these essays to learn from and identify with. In these essays you may find a mirror of your own journey.

The writers explain in engaging detail how this approach enriched and refreshed their enquiry and their established practice, be it Sufism, Buddhism, Christianity, Western philosophy, Advaita Vedanta, Perennialism or 'new age'.

As Greg Goode writes in the introduction, *Readers may find it a useful springboard to look at nonduality from different angles or learn that someone else is experiencing the same issues they are going through.*

Paperback | $9.45/£7.50 | 5.5" x 8.5" | 192p

'WHAT THE...'
A Conversation About Living

by Darryl Bailey

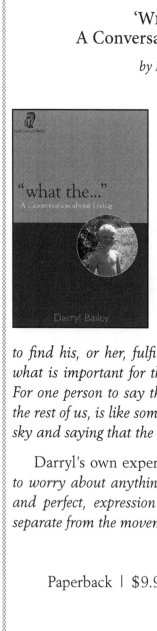

After a long break from writing, Darryl returns with an in-depth examination of his own journey, both inner and outer, spanning a period of 54 years, with time spent in four countries. He has been a Buddhist monk and a factory worker, he has learned and he has taught, he has suffered, he has enjoyed... and he has found that: *For each apparent person to find his, or her, fulfilment, they will have to feel out what is important for them, in their unique situation... For one person to say that there's something wrong with the rest of us, is like someone stepping out under the night sky and saying that the stars aren't arranged properly.*

Darryl's own experience taught him: *I didn't have to worry about anything... Everything was the natural, and perfect, expression of existence. I wasn't anything separate from the movement of existence itself.*

Paperback | $9.95/£7.95 | 5 x 8" | 104p

THE FREEDOM TO LOVE—The Life and Vision of Catherine Harding

by Karin Visser

The Freedom to Love is the story of Catherine Harding. She is a remarkable woman who has lived, loved and lost through remarkable and momentous times—as a child in occupied France and, after WWII, in Paris when: *Lots of funny and enjoyable things happened to us in Paris, but we were always hungry!*

She has travelled the world to meet profound and original thinkers and teachers, raised five children and worked to support them. In 1991 she was persuaded to attend a Headless Way workshop presented by the English philosopher and mystic Douglas Harding. Subsequently she worked with Douglas to introduce people around the world to the art of 'Seeing' until Douglas' death in 2007. A number of Douglas' 'experiments' are appended to *The Freedom to Love* for readers to try for themselves.

Catherine has been skilfully and sensitively interviewed by Karin Visser to produce a book that is thought-provoking, down to earth and inspiring.

Paperback | $13.95/£10.45 | 5.5" x 8.5" | 166p

THE TEN THOUSAND THINGS

by Robert Saltzman

A new and more affordable edition of the acclaimed book, *The Ten Thousand Things* by Robert Saltzman. This edition is text-only, without the photographs contained in the first edition.

"You do not have to believe anything in order to be alive. Like the stars in the sky, this aliveness is present whether noticed or not, and when the contraction called "myself" relaxes sufficiently, the aliveness feels obvious and indisputable. That relaxation of the clenched "myself" feels like having been roused from a dream to find oneself alive and aware ... What is, simply is, and cannot become anything. Each moment feels fresh, different from any other, and entirely unspeakable. The future never arrives. Enlightenment is a non-issue—not worth thinking about. One simply experiences what living human beings experience from moment to moment, and that's it. And that is sufficient."

Paperback | $15.95/£12.50 | 5.5" x 8.5" | 230p

CONVERSATIONS ON NON-DUALITY

Twenty-Six Awakenings
edited by Eleanora Gilbert

The book explores the nature of true happiness, awakening, enlightenment and the 'Self' to be realised. It features 26 expressions of liberation, each shaped by different life experiences and offering a unique perspective.

The collection explores the different ways 'liberation' happened and 'suffering' ended. Some started with therapy, self-help workshops or read books written by spiritual masters, while others travelled to exotic places and studied with gurus. Others leapt from the despair of addiction to drugs and alcohol to simply waking up unexpectedly to a new reality.

The 26 interviews included in the book are with: David Bingham, Daniel Brown, Sundance Burke, Katie Davis, Peter Fenner, Steve Ford, Jeff Foster, Suzanne Foxton, Gangaji, Richard Lang, Roger Linden, Wayne Liquorman, Francis Lucille, Mooji, Catherine Noyce, Jac O'Keeffe, Tony Parsons, Bernie Prior, Halina Pytlasinska, Genpo Roshi, Florian Schlosser, Mandi Solk, Rupert Spira, James Swartz, Richard Sylvester and Pamela Wilson.

CONSCIOUS.TV / Cherry Red Books

Printed in Great Britain
by Amazon